VICTORIAN VERSE

A Guide for Edexcel AS/A Level English Literature
(9ET0/03)

About the Author

After graduating from Oxford University with a degree in English Language and Literature, and 26 years working for British Airways, I decided to train as a teacher of English. For the next ten years, I taught in the secondary state sector in a multi-cultural and socio-economically diverse area west of London. On my retirement in 2016, I was second in the English department, co-ordinator of the A Level English Literature curriculum and Lead Year 13 tutor, co-ordinating university entrance applications. I am also an Examiner for AQA GCSE English Literature.

My approach to studying poetry is straightforward: unless you understand *what is happening* in the poem – the event, incident or story – about which the poet weaves his literary magic, there can be no understanding of a poet's literary techniques. The two are inextricably intertwined. There is a LOT of very variable analysis of poetry on the internet. Much of it stems from a failure to understand *what is happening*. This failure leads to the kind of nonsense that leaves students with a rattle-bag of literary terminology but with nothing on which to hang it. Naming metric forms and rhyme schemes, and poetic techniques such as *assonance* and *sibilance*, with no understanding of why the poet has used them, is a waste of time. It also leads to the kind of spurious, and erroneous, analysis of structure and form. I have read, in exam papers, that the *"shape of the line on the page, if you turn it sideways, corresponds to the furrows of a field."* Or, *"the varied line length suggests the outline of the Manhattan skyline"*. Students do not come up with ideas like this unless there is a fundamental failure to grasp the links between *substance (*the *"what is happening")* and *form (*rhythm and rhyme) and *language (*the words used*)*.

This guide is an attempt to make these links and help students appreciate why a poem has been written in the way that it has.

Contents

About this Guide 1

The Victorians – Age of Paradox 5

The Victorian Way of Death 15

Bibliography 17

A Note on Themes 18

"In Memoriam – A.H.H" – Alfred, Lord Tennyson 22

VII – "Dark house…" 23

XCV – "By night we linger'd on the lawn" 26

"Maud" – Alfred, Lord Tennyson 32

I.xi – "O let the solid ground" 32

I.xviii – "I have led her home…" 35

I. xxii – "Come into the garden, Maud" 43

II.iv – "O that 'twere possible" 51

Introduction to the Brontes 59

"The Visionary" – Emily and Charlotte Bronte 60

"Grief" – Elizabeth Barrett Browning 64

From "Sonnets from the Portuguese" – XX1V – Elizabeth Barrett Browning 67

"The Best Thing in the World" – Elizabeth Barrett Browning 70

"Died…" – Elizabeth Barrett Browning 74

"My Last Duchess" – Robert Browning 81

"Home-Thoughts, from Abroad" – Robert Browning 90

"Meeting at Night" – Robert Browning 95

"Love in a Life" – Robert Browning 98

"The Autumn day its course has run" – Charlotte Bronte...101

"The house was still –..." – Charlotte Bronte 103

"I now had only to retrace" – Charlotte Bronte 105

"The Nurse believed ..." – Charlotte Bronte 109

Stanzas - "Often rebuked..." – Charlotte or Emily Bronte ...110

"Remember" – Christina Rossetti............113

"Echo" – Christina Rossetti 116

"May" – Christina Rossetti 120

"A Birthday" – Christina Rossetti 122

"Somewhere or Other" – Christina Rossetti............126

"At an Inn" – Thomas Hardy 128

"I Look into my Glass" – Thomas Hardy 133

"Drummer Hodge" – Thomas Hardy 136

"A Wife in London" - Thomas Hardy 141

"The Darkling Thrush" – Thomas Hardy............146

About this Guide

The Guide has been written primarily for students of A Level English Literature as specified by Edexcel in the post-2015 syllabus (9ET0). It addresses Component 3 (9ET0/3) – Poetry, specifically, the requirement to study a "literary period".

The Guide covers all the poems in the literary period "The Victorians" as selected from *"The New Oxford Book of Victorian Verse"*, Editor Christopher Ricks (OUP, 2008).

The Guide aims to address all the Assessment Objectives for the examination of this component, namely:

AO1 - Articulate creative, informed and relevant responses to literary texts, using appropriate terminology and concepts, and coherent, accurate written expression.

AO2 - Demonstrate detailed critical understanding in analysing the ways in which structure, form and language shape meanings in literary texts.

AO3 - Demonstrate understanding of the significance and influence of the contexts in which literary texts are written and received

The poems are explored individually, but links and connections between them are drawn as appropriate. The format of each exploration is similar:

- An overview of relevant contextual factors, such as biographical, social-economic, political and literary
- An explanation of any key features of the poem that require additional explanation or illustration
- A brief summary of the metric form and rhyme scheme
- A "walk-through" (or explication) of the poem, ensuring that what is happening in the poem is understood, how

the rhythm and rhyme contribute to meaning, an explanation of the meaning of words which may be unfamiliar, an exploration of imagery and language and a comment on main themes.

A note on "appropriate terminology" (AO1)

This means the use of the semantic field of literary criticism – or "jargon". Criticism has a language to describe the features peculiar to the study of literature, just as football has words to describe manoeuvres and equipment – *"penalty"*, *"off-side"*, *"wing"*, *"long cross"*, *"throw-in"*. To be able to critique literature, you need to know this language and use it correctly. Throughout this guide, literary terminology has been *italicised*, indicating that these words need to become part of your vocabulary when discussing the texts and writing essays. For illustration, here are some very basic literary terms that are often carelessly used and will lose you marks in the exam if you do not apply them correctly.

Text – is the printed words. The *whole text* is all the words that are identified, usually by a *title*, as belonging together as an integral piece of writing.
A *Book* is a collection of printed pages bound together to make a *whole text.* A *book* can be any text – fiction, non-fiction; play, novel; car maintenance manual, encyclopaedia. A *book* is a **physical** entity, like *"DVD"* or *"scroll"*, not a creative one.
A *novel* is a particular kind of text – a *genre*. It is characterised by certain creative features, such as being *fictional,* usually *narrative in structure* and with various *characters* who do things, or have things happen to them. It may be *descriptive*, and may contain *dialogue*.
A *play* is another *genre*. It is designed to be performed and watched, rather than read. It can be *fictional* or *non-fictional*, or a mixture. It is predominantly made up of *dialogue* between

characters, although there may be descriptive elements within this *dialogue* and in the *stage directions*.

A *poem* is a particular *genre* which is characterised by the deliberate, and recurring, use of *rhythm* and *rhyme* and/or by a particular attention to *diction*, in the form of *word-choice* and *imagery*. It is opposed to *prose*. However, there are *poetical* prose writers whose language uses the distinctive features of poetry – such as *alliteration*, *rhythm* and *imagery*.

Beyond these simple definitions, there is a host of other, more technical language. This language has been used where it helps to describe features of the texts and is defined where it is used on the first usage, and subsequently when repeated, depending on how common the usage. So, *alliteration* has been defined on its first use; *iambic tetrametre* has been defined repeatedly, as its usage is less familiar.

A note on "shape meaning" (AO2)

There are very few marks to be gained by simply spotting and correctly naming literary techniques. Comments on literary techniques **must** be linked to purpose and meaning to gain marks in the higher bands. This principle has been followed in the analyses of the texts. See the section *"About the Author"* for a further comment on the dangers of spotting literary techniques in isolation from the meaning of the text. Not all literary techniques used receive a comment; only those that are particularly relevant to the discussion of meaning, form or theme have been explored.

A note on "contexts" (AO3)

The new specification marks a shift in the approach to "context" emphasising the need to link contextual factors to the texts, so as to inform understanding and analysis. Therefore, this guide does not pretend to give a comprehensive biographical, social-economic, political or literary history of the Victorians. A wealth of information is readily available on websites and in history texts and suggestions for further reading and research are given throughout. However, there is an introductory chapter on the main pre-occupations of the Victorian period to give some understanding of the key concerns of writers during the period. It is necessarily broad and generalised.

The Victorians – Age of Paradox

Queen Victoria ruled for a long time – 1847 - 1901. Her 63-year reign has only been surpassed, in England, and now the world (with the death of the King of Thailand in October 2016) by the present Queen Elizabeth II. Much can happen in 63 years. Going back 63 years from today to the 1950s: there were no computers, no mobile phones; air travel was limited to the rich few; divorce and single parents were a social taboo; no-one had sex before marriage (or admitted to it); the contraceptive pill did not exist and condoms were sold under the counter; homosexual acts between men were illegal (they had never been illegal between women); immigration was a new phenomenon - notices were posted outside hotels and rented accommodation saying "*No Blacks, No Irish, No Dogs*"; people still went regularly to church, whatever their private beliefs; children were baptised into the Christian faith as a matter of course; church weddings were the norm; the school-leaving age was 15; 3% of students obtained university degrees, compared with more than 30% in 2000.

Can you imagine such a world? Well, the Victorian era saw a similar revolution in technology, sexual politics, the concept of Empire, religion and education. It was an era of turbulence and questioning. Writers were at the forefront in coming to terms with these shifts in perception – they were often the first to articulate what the changing cultural landscape would mean to the population as a whole and many of them led the demand for change. Their writing reflects the paradoxes at the heart of Victorian society. These can be summarised:

OLD	NEW
Religious	Scientific
God	Man
The Family Unit	Empire
Rural Life	Industry
Extreme Poverty	Wealth Creation

Religious/Scientific

Although the 18th century had seen major advancements in scientific discovery and an increasing belief in the supremacy of rational thought over religious orthodoxy, in what has become known as The Age of Enlightenment, the Victorians were still a society steeped in religious observance and ritual. There was a spate of building and rebuilding churches to accommodate the growth in population, particularly in the cities, and monies voted by Parliament to support this building programme. "Victorian values" were based on the teachings of the Bible, including adherence to the Ten Commandments, which shaped Victorian attitudes towards sexual relationships, marriage, death and the existence of an after-life.

However, there was an increasing secularisation of society that paralleled advancements in a scientific understanding of the world. Two developments are illustrative of the seismic shift in (educated) people's world view – the study of fossils and rocks by James Hutton and others, and the publication of Darwin's "*Origin of Species*" in 1859, followed by "*The Descent of Man*" in 1871. James Hutton's study of geology in the late 18th century, popularised by Charles Lyell in the mid-19th century, challenged the widely-held belief that the earth was created less than 10,000 years ago, as those believed who took a literal reading of the creation of the world in Genesis, the first book of the Old Testament. His studies suggested that the world was continuously forming and reforming and had been doing so for millions of years. Charles Darwin read the works of Charles Lyell during the second voyage of *"The Beagle"*, a five-year mission to the south Atlantic and Pacific. This, together with his own research, led to his theory of evolution by natural selection. This blew apart the creation myth and with it, the bedrock of religious belief. The Victorians, exposed to these revolutionary ideas through increased access to education and mass production of pamphlets, broadsheets and books, found themselves beset by doubts.

God/Man

If God created Man, then God is the centre of Man's world. He, with his only begotten Son, Christ, is the *"alpha et omega"*. Life revolves around His teachings; society behaves according to His laws. Man is also placed "in dominion" over the "beasts of the fields and fowls of the air". By extrapolation, Man, specifically Christian Man, also holds dominion over the non-believer – all those who are NOT Christian. Also, God made Man in His image. His image is White. Those not in His image and not of His Church are, by definition, inferior and need to be "brought to God". The Righteousness of the Victorians and their missionary zeal can be seen in the words of a notable hymn *"Hills of the North, rejoice!"* (1865) which reassures far-flung parts of the world that their time of waiting is over and Christianity has arrived to save them. It is also the era of the missionary work of, amongst others, David Livingstone, who saw Britain's liberal imperialism as an indivisible combination of "commerce and Christianity".

With the veracity of the Bible in question, and hence, a questioning of the very existence of a God, writers and philosophers increasingly turned to Man, and Man's intellectual curiosity, as the guide on how to live one's life. The Enlightenment avowed the supremacy of the intellect. *Atheism* or "no Gods" was a feature of the French Revolution (1789-98), the cataclysmic, brutal and bloody overthrow of the French monarchical system that sent shockwaves across Europe. The word *"agnostic"* was first coined in 1869 by T H Huxley, a champion of Darwin, to characterise his methodology: – *"In matters of the intellect, follow your reason as far as it will take you, without regard to any other consideration... In matters of the intellect, do not pretend that conclusions are certain which are not demonstrated or demonstrable."* The idea of "humanism" or the cult of humanity, as opposed to the cult of God, gained traction during the century. The end of the century saw Sigmund Freud's *"Interpretation of Dreams"* and the birth of psychoanalysis. Man begins to take centre stage.

The Family Unit/Empire

Queen Victoria was not just the Queen of England – she was Empress of India, the Mother of the Empire. In her was embodied the ideal of womanhood, motherhood and majesty. She came to the throne aged 18 and married her first-cousin, Prince Albert of Saxe-Coburg and Gotha, aged 21. She had nine children, who established a wide-flung dynasty in Europe, earning Victoria the soubriquet "grandmother of Europe". Her early reign was full of mishap: she falsely accused a lady-in-waiting of being pregnant, which became a public scandal; she survived a number of assassination attempts; she was poorly advised by her ministers. However, her marriage to Prince Albert, with whom she fell instantly in love on their first meeting, was the celebrity marriage to which others aspired. It was Queen Victoria who started the fashion of wearing white for a wedding and having a tiered wedding cake. It was Prince Albert, who was German, who popularised the Christmas tree, erecting one in Windsor Castle in 1848. When they sat together for an early photograph, in 1860, women copied her dress and men began to wear their hair and moustache like Prince Albert's. When the queen went into mourning on the death of Albert in 1861, the nation followed suit.

The Royal Family embodied, particularly for the middle-class, the ideal, nuclear family.

This family placed the man at the centre of the middle-class household, with women relegated to *"the domestic sphere"*. This separation of the roles of the sexes was relatively new – when "work" was largely carried out within the home, men and women worked alongside one another and the woman would have had a role in sustaining the family as an economic, as well as domestic, unit. However, with work increasingly taking place in spaces outside the domestic sphere, men were absent from the household during the day, in offices and factories, leaving the women confined to the home. Their role was to support the husband, raise the children, and manage the servants. A middle-class household would have had at least one domestic servant. Contraception was unreliable and infant mortality high. The failure of one, and fear of the other, led to large families which required full-time attention. Maintaining a stable, warm and well-fed household was a valued role.

It was not usual for middle-class women to work until later in the century, although women who were unmarried, had no private wealth, and could not live with their parents, took places as governesses and school-teachers, but were, in effect, little more than domestic servants. This is a recurrent theme in the literature of the time. However, women were becoming increasingly educated, and with exposure to new ideas came demands for equality. The Married Woman's Property Act, allowing women to own property which previously they would have had to hand over to their husbands, was passed in 1897. Working class women worked alongside men in the new factories and textile mills, often in appalling conditions. Change for them was slower in coming.

Sobriety, propriety, the sanctity of marriage and the supremacy of the family unit were the middle-class values on which the Empire was built, coupled with a work ethic embedded in Protestantism, which valued hard work, discipline and frugality. Supremacy in manufacturing, a commitment to free trade, the strength of its navy and the weakening of traditional mercantile and naval enemies, such as the Spanish and Dutch, as well as the defeat of France in the Napoleonic wars, established Britain as the premier world power, instigating a period known as the *Pax Britannica,* (*"British peace"*), with Britain as the "global policeman". When Victoria came to the throne, Britain already ruled Canada, parts of the Caribbean, Australia and New Zealand, much of India and small parts of Africa and South America. From the 1870s, control was extended to Egypt, parts of east Africa and southern Africa, to eventually encompass more than a quarter of the world's population and a fifth of its area. The Great Exhibition of 1851, devised by Prince Albert, and held in Hyde Park in a vast glasshouse designed by John Paxton, was the first World's Fair, to showcase the wealth of the Empire. Six million people – a third of the population – attended the Exhibition.

Although there was only one European war during the period, to resist Russian influence in the Crimea extending through the Middle-East, building Empire did not come entirely without conflict. Local insurrections amongst the colonised were suppressed, as in the Indian Mutiny of 1857, and the Boer Wars of 1880/81 and 1899-1902 which advanced British interests in the gold and diamond mines of southern Africa.

Rural Life/Industry

Prior to the "Industrial Revolution", Britain was largely an agrarian economy – one based on the production of materials from the countryside, primarily food and wool. Wool and cotton (the latter imported from the slave plantations of America) formed the basis of British trade up until the late 18th century. Textile manufacture took place primarily in "cottage industries" – the production of goods on a small, local scale, often by individual craftsmen and women, loosely bound together by local agreements with merchants. Improvements in agricultural techniques during the 17th and 18th centuries improved agricultural efficiency, much needed to cope with a growing population, but it also meant fewer people were required to work on the farms. Few owned their own farms, which were largely in the hands of the aristocracy or landowners who had purchased their estates with riches acquired from trade in the expanding Empire.

"The Industrial Revolution" is the name given to the period between, roughly, the mid-18th century and the middle of the 19th century which shifted Britain from an economy based on agriculture to one based on manufacturing. It was made possible by a series of inventions and developments in, particularly, textiles, steam power and iron making. Taken together, these inventions and developments in engineering replaced the cottage industries and led to a move of the majority of the population away from the countryside into the towns where the new factories were often sited. By 1851, half the population of Britain lived in towns. This shift led to considerable social challenges, including pressure on housing, sanitation and water provision. It also required changes to traditional working patterns which, in a rural environment (largely determined by the cycle of day and night and the seasons) had been the norm, but, in an industrial setting, imposed terrible hardships on men, women and children – long hours without respite, seven days a week working and children working in mines and factories at a very young age. Working in the new textile mills was dangerous – there were no safety regulations and scant regard for the loss of life or limb. Workers suffered terrible injuries attempting to maintain working machinery or in mining accidents. During the early 19th century, a series of acts were passed to increasingly limit the amount of days and hours the more vulnerable were required to work.

Transportation at this time also underwent a revolution. Horse-drawn conveyances for transporting goods gradually gave way, first, to water transport by canal and then land transport by railway – the development of which put Britain at the forefront of global trade and created new industries, as well as necessitating "standard time". The Victorians "invented" the seaside – a place for the urban masses to get out of the smog of the big cities and breathe fresh air.

Extreme Poverty/Wealth Creation

The social hierarchy of Victorian Britain was rigidly demarcated. There were three broad bands: the upper-classes, who were the aristocratic, titled, land-owners; the expanding middle-class, who were professionals and "white collar" workers – merchants, mill-owners, doctors, lawyers, office workers, army offices and officers of the church; the manual labourers - agricultural labourers, who worked on the land, but did not own the land, and those who worked in the factories. There was also a growing tide of "urban poor" – people who had flocked to the cities in search of work and lived a precarious existence on the edge of society. Mobility between the classes was limited; the "unsuitability" of marriages between men and women of a different class is a recurring literary theme. It is dangerous to generalise about Victorian "society" as there was a significant difference between the lives of the different social classes and a huge gulf between rich and poor. Many writers of the 19th century concerned themselves with the "plight of the poor", but equally, their concerns are those of the educated middle-class.

Victorian Britain had no "welfare state". The poor were the responsibility of the church parishes who looked after those too ill, old or feeble to work and with no means of support. Otherwise, they begged, relying on the charity of individuals. There had always been the "rural poor", who were dependent on seasonal work, but as work in agriculture declined and as populations increased, the burden became increasingly hard for the churches to bear. Some parishes banded together to build "Poor Houses", institutions where those unable to find work and support their families were required to go. In return for board and lodging, they worked in the Poor House and surrounding farms. The regime was harsh, and families were separated. Many ran away, preferring to beg. In 1834, the new Poor Laws introduced the "Workhouse", run along similar lines and equally detested. Threats of being "put in the Workhouse" were still made to children over a century later. The situation in towns and cities was worse. Mass migration, coupled with population growth, led to chronic overcrowding in urban centres, bringing prostitution, disease and crime. Work, when available, was paid at subsistence levels and subject to seasonal fluctuations. By 1900, nearly a third of women were employed as servants in domestic households, working long hours with little or no time off. There were no employment rights. Charles Dickens is the supreme chronicler of the life of the urban poor and working class in London, whilst Henry Mayhew produced detailed etchings of the workers themselves, collected in his *"London Labour and London Poor"* of 1851.

In contrast, Victorian Britain saw the rise of the middle-class, as trade with the Empire expanded and manufacturing and commerce demanded an army of literate clerks, office keepers and managers to handle all aspects of the manufacturers' and merchants' global businesses. New technologies, such as the telegraph and the telephone, demanded people to operate them. Teacher-training was introduced in 1846. Building and maintaining an Empire demanded officers in the army; the Church required missionaries to spread the Gospel. In addition to an army of street-sellers who supplied urban dwellers with food and small manufactured goods, middle-class women could go to new shops, staffed with both men and women, to examine goods imported from all over the globe and to the new department stores to buy their clothes – previously made by hand at home.

The demand for "blue" and "white collar" workers – those who did not work with their hands in manual labour and with more than basic literacy – led to changes in the education system. The nobility and gentry had enjoyed access to the "public" (rather than "monastic") schools for hundreds of years, as well as private tutoring. The aspirations of the new middle class towards a higher level of education led to a spate of new institutions being founded during the 19th century. Universal education was, at first, haphazard, with a network of Ragged Schools, Parish Schools, Church Schools and apprenticeships supplying education at a basic level. Not until 1880 was universal education provided until the age of 13.

The Victorian Way of Death

Death, and the fear of death, was an ever-present concern of Victorian writers. Whilst quoting average life-expectancy figures needs to be treated with caution, (as it is skewed by high rates of infant mortality and the death of women in childbirth), the average life-expectancy of a baby born in a large town early in the century was around 35 years. By the middle of the century, it had dropped to between 25 – 30 years. One in five children born during the 1830s – 40s died before their 5th birthday. Particularly for the urban poor, poverty and malnutrition, coupled with diseases such as cholera and tuberculosis, in over-crowded, unsanitary conditions, and high levels of violent crime, meant that death was ever-present. However, if you were lucky enough to survive beyond 40 years, then you might look to live almost as long as people today.

Funerals were big business in mid-Victorian Britain. In *"Oliver Twist"*, Dickens gives us a picture of the fetishising of death that grew up during the period. Oliver obtains a post as a "Mute" – a person who stands silently by the coffin and accompanies it to the churchyard. He is a part of the elaborate funeral rites that even Victorians of modest means arranged, together with the black-plumed horses and glass coffins. There was an industry, not just of funeral directors, but of the accompanying "accessories": black mourning clothes; mourning jewellery, often made of jet from Whitby in Yorkshire; black-edged stationery; garlands and black ribbons for decorating houses and churches. With the growth in population and move to cities, the old, local churchyards were soon over-flowing. To relieve the pressure for burial space in London, the Victorians opened a ring of cemeteries outside the city – Highgate, Kensal Green, Brompton, Abney Park, West Norwood, Nunhead and Tower Hamlets were all built between 1832 and 1841. This was the era of the monumental mason – the men who carved the angels, urns, books and cherubs to stand at the head of gravestones, much of which reflected the architecture of the Gothic revival.

No surprise, then, that Death and the trappings of death infuse the writings of novelists and poets of the period. This preoccupation stems not just from a melancholy streak in the writers, but from their everyday experience. Many were directly touched by the deaths of loved ones close to them. Dickens had a sister who died aged five, his beloved sister-in-law died at the age of seventeen. Many of Dickens' characters die young – Little Nell in *"The Old Curiosity Shop"*, Smyke in *"Nicholas Nickleby"*, Joe in *"Bleak House"*. The poets in the selection were similarly touched by death. Tennyson's friend Arthur Hallam died at the age of 22; the Brontes lost their mother and aunt when they were young and their brother in his 20s, they all died before the age of 40; two of EBB's brothers died when she was in her twenties and she was in ill-health most of her life; Christina Rossetti also suffered an undiagnosed malady and lived in constant fear of early death, although she survived to 64. The Brontes' novels are full of dying people: Jane Eyre is an orphan; her friend Helen Burns dies at Lowood House; Francis and Catherine Earnshaw die under the age of 20 as does Linton Heathcliff. The poetry in the selection has Death as a recurring theme: *"In Memoriam – AHH"*; *Maud*'s brother is killed violently; *"Died.."* is about a death notice; *"My Last Duchess"* has a dead woman at its heart; *"Love in a Life"* is haunted by the idea of a lost loved one; *"The Nurse"* is visiting a dead or dying man; *"Remember"* is written from the point of view of a woman contemplating her own death; in *"Echo"*, there are images of death; *"Drummer Hodge"* and *"A Wife in London"* are about men killed in War.

For the Victorians, the words of the Burial Service, "*In the midst of life we are in death*", were very real.

Bibliography

Key Concepts in Victorian Literature – Sean Purchase – Palgrave Key Concepts (2006) 978-1-4039-3210-7
Victorian Poetry in Context – Rosie Miles – Bloomsbury (2013) 978-0-8264-3767-9

The Victorian Web – www.victorianweb.org
The British Library – www.bl.uk
The Poetry Foundation – www.poetryfoundation.org
The Hardy Society – www.hardysociety.org
The Bronte Society – www.bronte.org.uk/about-us

Further links to useful websites are given in the text.

THE POEMS

A Note on Themes

The question in the A level examination for *Component 3 – Poetry Part B – Literary period* will be on a *"theme"* – a central concern or idea which may form the focus of the poem or be an integral part of its meaning. You will be asked to explore the presentation of this "theme" in one named poem and one other poem of your choice.

These "themes" could include, but not be limited to: an **emotion** – such as love, loss, sorrow, joy; the **evocation of "place"**, as the subject of the poem, or as the setting for the poem; the treatment of **abstract concepts** such as Time, or Death, or Religion; a **"happening"** such as War, Childhood, Marriage; the **relationships between men and women**. The range is very broad. Where a poem lends itself to suggesting a particular theme, this has been noted in the explication. However, these suggestions are not exhaustive; one of the skills to be mastered is to know the texts well enough to be able to link them to themes which may not be immediately obvious. In addition to this, there is one "theme" which seems to run through most of the selection, so it has been explored and illustrated below.

Liminal Spaces

Liminal means *"threshold"*, the part of a door that you step across to move from one space to another. *Liminality* is the space between different states – between night and day (dawn), between day and night (twilight), between life and death, between out and in, between sleeping and waking, as in dreams. Most of the poems in the selection are similarly concerned with situations where the poet/persona, or the setting, or the subject matter, or more than one of these, are "in between" states or spaces.

Tennyson

In *"In Memoriam – VII - Dark House"*, Tennyson seems unable to move on from the living presence of Hallam on the street he revisits, living in limbo, suspended between rejection of Hallam's death and realisation; *"XCV - By night we linger'd"* is set between night and day – a night when he seems to move from sorrow to reconciliation as dawn breaks; the *"Maud"* poems are full of liminal images – *"I.xi – O let the solid ground"* is set between the *"solid ground"* and *"sweet heavens"*; *"I.xviii - I have led her home"* is set at the point where Maud is both "his" and "not his" – he is on the verge of a consummation of their love, but it is never realised; Maud does not *"Come into the Garden"* – we leave the narrator still waiting; *"II.iv - O that 'twere possible"* imagines Maud as a ghost, caught between life and death and the narrator as a confused *"wasted frame"*.

Emily & Charlotte Bronte – The Visionary

The setting is inside, but the focus is on the visitor coming through the winter weather to visit her. She, too, is in a "limbo", where the Visionary is anticipated (as in *"Come into the garden, Maud"*) but not yet realised.

Elizabeth Barrett Browning

"Grief" explores the emotion of the title, with a central image of a statue, life-*like*, but dead and unable to "move on"; The subject of *"Died..."* is both alive and dead at the same time; they are talking about him as if alive, even as his obituary notice travels to them from London. This *dichotomy*[1] recurs in Hardy's *"A Wife in London"*.

---

[1] Contradictory position

Robert Browning

The Duke in *"My Last Duchess"* is, literally, "between" Duchesses; In *"Home Thoughts…"*, the poet is in Italy but casting his thoughts toward England, and is thus caught between the two; the focus of *"Meeting at Night"* is in the space between "not with the beloved" and "with the beloved"; In *"Love in a Life"* the focus is on the emptiness between the beloved being "not found" and "found" and remains unresolved.

Charlotte Bronte

All of the poems in the selection by Charlotte Bronte are set in *liminal space*. *"The Autumn day"* is set at Twilight: *"The house was still…"* is also set at twilight, and the birds' songs occupy the space between indoors (the canary) and outdoors (the free bird); *"I now had only to retrace"* recounts the point at which the poet turns back from her outward walk to head for home; *"The Nurse believed…"* has a question at its heart – is the man alive or dead?; *"Stanzas"* opens with a statement that puts the poet in a space between the world of the imagination and the real world.

Christina Rossetti

"Remember" explores memory – the place where the dead still exist for the living and the first stanza shows the poet *"half turn to go yet turning stay".*; an *"Echo"* exists in the space between the first sound and the return (as in the songs between the birds in *"The house was still"*) and the poem ends with a wish for a *"dream"* where the lover returns; *"May"* captures the very moment when she *"passes"* from a feeling of hope and joy to one of desolation, as Tennyson does in reverse in *XCV*; *"Somewhere or other"* by its title suggests that the poet is caught between anticipation and consummation with only a *"hedge between"*.

Thomas Hardy

In *"At the Inn"*, the poet describes the two *"As we seemed we were not"* – they existed as lovers, to the innkeeper, but were not, lovers and yet not lovers (like the alive/dead man in *"Died..."* or in *"The Nurse..."*); In *"I Look into My Glass"*, a mirror is a space between the reality and the reflection in the mirror, where Hardy seems to exist as both young, on the inside, and old, on the outside; even *"Drummer Hodge"* seems to lie between England, where he was born, and Africa, where his body is, as if a bit of England has been transported out there; *"A wife in London"* captures the time between receiving notice of her husband's death and a letter written in the dead man's hand – again, there was a moment where he was both alive AND dead; *"The Darkling Thrush"* is set at the turn of the year and the turn of the century – New Year's Eve, 1899. A liminal space indeed.

"In Memoriam – A.H.H" – Alfred, Lord Tennyson

In Memoriam is an *elegy* – a poem which mourns someone's death. The form originated in Greece and classical elegies follow a set structure in response to the death –*lament* (crying and wailing), *eulogy* (praise of the dead person), followed by *reconciliation* (consolation and solace) with the fact of death and, often, hope of a better life to come. There are elements of this tri-partite structure in Tennyson's long poem.

The poem was written over 16 years, following the death of Arthur Hallam, aged 22, whom Tennyson had met up at Cambridge. Hallam was also a poet, and they had competed for the same prize, which Tennyson won. Hallam was engaged to Tennyson's sister, Emily, at the time of his death. Hallam's death was the defining moment of Tennyson's life and he returns to it, not just in the poem dedicated to him, but in many others, including *"Ulysses"* and, arguably, *"Tithonus"*, a *dramatic monologue*[2] spoken by a mortal given eternal life, but not eternal youth, by a goddess.

Their friendship has been described as *"swift and deep"* (C. Ricks, *Tennyson*, 1972). Inevitably, modern readers will consider whether their relationship was homosexual, by inclination, if not in practice. Perhaps intense, close friendships between heterosexual men are less common today, and less understood, now that women are part of men's social sphere from an early age. Similar friendships between women would probably go unremarked.

---

[2] A *dramatic monologue* is a poem where the poet takes on the role or voice of another person, not himself.

VII – "Dark house..."

This first extract in the selection is from the early part of the poem and could be categorised as a *lament* – the focus is on how Tennyson feels in the aftermath of his loss. He is not yet sufficiently detached from the initial shock and grief to be able to either praise his friend or be comforted. It is raw and painful. Compare this extract with number *CXIX* which comes late in the sequence. Although it starts in the same way, note the difference in emotion; there is a feeling of consolation or peace in the later extract.

The whole of *"In Memoriam"* is written in *iambic tetrametre* – lines with four *iambic* (unstressed/stressed – ti-**TUM**) beats, with a consistent rhyme scheme *abba*. This heightens the feeling of obsession as it is relentless. However, variation is created by the use of *enjambment (*running the sense of a sentence or phrase over the end of a line and onto the next*)* and *caesura (*pausing the line in the middle*)*, which gives the poem forward momentum and allows for changes in pace and emphasis, to reflect shifts in emotion.

Tennyson revisits the house where Hallam used to live. He cannot sleep, so comes at night to mourn unseen.

Dark house, by which once more I stand
Here in the long unlovely street,
Doors, where my heart was used to beat
So quickly, waiting for a hand,

He opens with a direct address to the *personified*[3] "*house*" and, in line 3, the "*Doors*". He is asking these inanimate objects to look at him, an object of pity – "*Behold me*" (line 6); the *personification* emphasises the emptiness of the house ("*Dark*" because Hallam is

---

[3] *Personification* is to attribute human characteristics to objects

absent, as well as it being at night) and the contrast with the former welcome he received from Hallam at this house whilst he was alive. Notice, too, the *enjambment* ("*beat/so quickly*") emphasising his former emotions. The *alliteration* of "*long, unlovely*" in line two is typical Tennyson. A*lliteration*, the repetition of letters at the beginning of words that are close together in the text, is one of his favourite techniques. See it also in the last line of the extract. The street is "*unlovely*", now that Hallam is not on it.

The use of *anaphora* (repetition) is another feature of Tennyson. He uses "*a hand/A hand*" to link the two stanzas, to contrast his former meetings with Hallam and the present absence. Everything is the same – the house, the door - and yet utterly changed by death.

A hand that can be clasp'd no more—
Behold me, for I cannot sleep,
And like a guilty thing I creep
At earliest morning to the door.

In his description of himself as "*a guilty thing*", there is a sense that he is aware of the extreme of his grief; is it normal? People do, however, go back to places where they experienced happier times when they are in mourning.

He is not here; but far away
The noise of life begins again,
And ghastly thro' the drizzling rain
On the bald street breaks the blank day.

"*He is not here*" is an echo from the New Testament. These are the words the Angel said to Mary Magdalene when she found Christ's tomb empty and later mistakes Jesus for the gardener. This is evidence of Tennyson's worship of Hallam – there are other images of him as Christ-like in the long poem. The use of *caesura* in this line is deceptive; on first reading it seems as if "*but far away"* is set in opposition to *"He is not here"*. However, the *enjambment* links it to *"the noise of life"*, thus serving two purposes. Life *"begins again"*, in spite of the death, but is reduced to *"noise"* only – sound without meaning. A similar idea can be found in *"Macbeth"* – life is *"a tale/Told by an idiot, full of sound and fury,/Signifying nothing."*

Tennyson uses *pathetic fallacy*[4] to project his feelings of life being now meaningless onto the weather (*"drizzling rain"*). *"ghastly"* is used here close to the modern meaning of *"awful"* but also with the older meaning of *"terrifying"* which is closely related to *"ghost"* – an example of multiple layering of meaning in a single word.

The last line is one of the most famous lines in Tennyson's poetry. Note the *alliteration*[5] of the *"b"* and the use of mono-syllabic words - like an echoing knock on the door; the use of *personification* – the street is *"bald"*, as in devoid of life, the day is *"blank"* – empty and lifeless. But the use of *"blank"* is also *hypallage*[6] (or a *"transferred epithet"*) – the transference of Tennyson's emotions to the street, now that it is devoid of Hallam.

---

[4] *Pathetic fallacy* is to attribute human emotions to the weather or the surroundings, as if they were in sympathy
[5] *Alliteration* is using words with the same first letter or combination of letters in words that are in close proximity. They do not have to be next to each other.
[6] *Hypallage*, or *transferred epithet*, is to use a word, often an adjective, to describe an inanimate object as having feelings which are actually being felt by the poet/persona.

XCV – "By night we linger'd[7] on the lawn"

This poem comes much later in the *"In Memoriam"* sequence and reflects an element of consolation and solace - the third phase of classical mourning. The raw grief of *"VII - Doors..."* - has given way to affectionate recollection and a more spiritual response to death. Tennyson wrote *"In Memoriam"* over more than fifteen years, gradually exploring and coming to terms with what the death of his friend meant to him at the spiritual, religious and moral level.

Tennyson has enjoyed a quiet evening with friends in a garden. There is little noise and it is warm. The scene is intensely realised, with faint sounds recorded. His friends go off to bed before him and, left alone, memories of Hallam return. He seems to hear, or seek his dead friend speaking to him in the fallen leaves - it is so vivid that at one point their souls seem to unite. Tennyson hears *"truths"* about the nature of Life, Faith, Love, Loss - he becomes in tune with spiritual matters - the *"pulsations"* of the world. As the vision fades, he doubts for a moment what it is he has learned or what he *"became"* when he seemed unified with the dead Hallam and the spirit of the world. But in that moment of doubt, a breeze blows across the garden as dawn breaks, bringing a promise of a new day. If nothing else, this gives him a tentative feeling of hope or progression.

This is weighty stuff. Tennyson himself admits that he can hardly put it into words. There is a mass of rather difficult writing on this poem on the internet, which is considered the climax of the whole sequence.

---

[7] The use of the apostrophe here and throughout – *linger'd* – is to show that the word is pronounced as two syllables rather than three – *lin-ge-red* - to maintain the rhythm.

By night we linger'd on the lawn,
For underfoot the herb was dry;
And genial warmth; and o'er the sky
The silvery haze of summer drawn;

The alliteration of *"linger'd on the lawn"* gives a feeling of drowsy indolence as the group of young men lounge around after dinner, smoking and drinking. Tennyson uses an archaic word, *"herb"*, for grass, harking back to the Romantic poets, writing earlier in the century. He places emphasis on the warmth of the summer evening; the *"silvery haze"* may be the stars which are so thick that they look like a mist over the night sky.

And calm that let the tapers burn
Unwavering: not a cricket chirr'd:
The brook alone far-off was heard,
And on the board the fluttering urn:

Tennyson emphasises the stillness and silence of the night with negatives: the tapers do not move (*"unwavering"*) and the crickets *onomatopoeic "chirr"* is not heard. It is so quiet and still that they can hear the sound of a distant stream and the *"fluttering"* noise of a (oil?) heater under a pot (*"urn"*) on the side table (*"board"*).

And bats went round in fragrant skies,
And wheel'd or lit the filmy shapes
That haunt the dusk, with ermine capes
And woolly breasts and beaded eyes;

Bats are wheeling around them catching moths. It is not entirely clear, because of the compactness of the writing, whether the *"filmy shapes"* are the bats or moths. The *"or lit"* in the second line suggests that he is referring to something other than the bats, and the *"haunt"* suggests the ghost-like whiteness of moths. *"Ermine"* is a white fur with black spots, made from the winter coat of stoats. Bats are not spotted black and white – some moths are, nor are bats *"filmy"*. Tennyson is quite particular in his descriptions of nature.

While now we sang old songs that peal'd
From knoll to knoll, where, couch'd at ease,
The white kine glimmer'd, and the trees
Laid their dark arms about the field.

The young men sing songs which ring out like bells across the hills, where white cattle (another archaic word used for romantic effect) lie in the grass, there coats glimmering in the starlight. The use of *"dark arms"* to personify the trees give a sense of safety and protection.

But when those others, one by one,
Withdrew themselves from me and night,
And in the house light after light
Went out, and I was all alone,

His friends gradually go off to bed, leaving him alone. The lights in the house are switched off one by one.

A hunger seized my heart; I read
Of that glad year which once had been,
In those fall'n leaves which kept their green,
The noble letters of the dead:

He is seized with a longing for Hallam. *"Read"* means he *"took meaning from"* the green leaves on the ground, a symbol of the youthful Hallam, who lies dead before his time, like the green (a symbol of life and growth) leaves on the grass. He reads a message from the dead man.

And strangely on the silence broke
The silent-speaking words, and strange
Was love's dumb cry defying change
To test his worth; and strangely spoke

The faith, the vigour, bold to dwell
On doubts that drive the coward back,
And keen thro' wordy snares to track
Suggestion to her inmost cell.

These two stanzas can be paraphrased as: surprised, the poet "hears" the words of the dead man break the *"silence"*. The dead man's love cries out in defiance of *"change"* (time? distance?) to test the strength (*"worth"*) of his love; his *"faith"* and *"vigour"* (life-force) speak out, showing his boldness in daring to doubt, or wonder, what happens to the dead. He is brave enough to follow trains of thought (*"wordy snares"*) that might even lead him to dark conclusions (*"inmost cell"*) about death (and by inference, faith and religion).

So word by word, and line by line,
The dead man touch'd me from the past,
And all at once it seem'd at last
The living soul was flash'd on mine,

He has interpreted the message from the dead Hallam. The *"at last"* suggests that this is the communication with Hallam that he has been seeking – at first, he missed his physical presence, but over time this has mutated into a more spiritual need, and this is the longed for communication.

And mine in his was wound, and whirl'd
About empyreal heights of thought,
And came on that which is, and caught
The deep pulsations of the world,

The poet feels that his soul and Hallam's have been bound together and have thought together and arrived at some universal truth (*"that which is"*). The *"is"* is a noun, not a verb, here. It means the truth of things, the *"deep pulsations"* which govern the world.

Aeonian music measuring out
The steps of Time--the shocks of Chance--
The blows of Death. At length my trance
Was cancell'd, stricken thro' with doubt.

These "*deep pulsations*" are likened to everlasting music - a reference to the "music of the spheres" which the heavens were believed to make as they rotated in harmony. This harmony is made up of three strands: *Time, Chance* and *Death*, to which all mankind is bound.

His moment of clarity is interrupted by an onslaught of doubt. Has he interpreted the message correctly?

Vague words! but ah, how hard to frame
In matter-moulded forms of speech,
Or ev'n for intellect to reach
Thro' memory that which I became:

He admits that it is difficult to express what he was transported into, in this moment of clarity as he became one with the dead Hallam, as it is beyond expressing in words. Words are designed to describe physical things ("*matter*"). It is difficult even to think, conceptualise, what has happened to him.

Till now the doubtful dusk reveal'd
The knolls once more where, couch'd at ease,
The white kine glimmer'd, and the trees
Laid their dark arms about the field;

But then something else happens - "(Un)*Till now*". Something has, or is about to change, that confirms his revelation. He recaps the opening scene of the poem; the hills are still there, the cows still "*glimmer'd*"; the trees still surround them protectively. But the "*dusk*" is now "*doubtful*" – it is giving way to something else. This is a similar technique to that used in *XCV*, where the outward appearance of things seems unchanged, and yet their meaning to the poet is changed utterly.

And suck'd from out the distant gloom
A breeze began to tremble o'er
The large leaves of the sycamore,
And fluctuate all the still perfume,

And gathering freshlier overhead,
Rock'd the full-foliaged elms, and swung
The heavy-folded rose, and flung
The lilies to and fro, and said,

A breeze blows up from the east, growing stronger as it moves over the sycamore trees, and the elm trees in the full leaf of summer, sending up the scents of the lilies and roses in the garden where the poet is sitting. Note the movement in the verbs and the growing intensity as the wind grows stronger: *"suck'd"*, *"tremble"*, *"fluctuate"*, *"Rock'd"*, *"swung"*, *"flung"*. Contrast this with the lazy verb *"linger'd"* of the first stanza, showing his growing confidence in the message being brought to him on the wind. Note also the imagery of full growth and bounty – the *"full-foliaged elms"* and *"heavy-folded rose"* – suggesting a spiritual fulfilment.

'The dawn, the dawn,' and died away;
And East and West, without a breath,
Mixt their dim lights, like life and death,
To broaden into boundless day.

The strengthening breeze brings the dawn, the mixing of the light in the east and the west. Resolution comes in the realisation that the world is a totality, there is both life and death, and that this enables him to move on. In the "boundless day" there is the possibility of hope for the future. Is it a religious Afterlife? It is an interpretation which the Victorians would have appreciated, but not necessarily one that Tennyson is advocating.

"Maud" – Alfred, Lord Tennyson

This long poem was described by Tennyson as a "*Monodrama*" - what we call a "*dramatic monologue*". The narrator is a persona created by Tennyson who tells us a (disjointed) story about the death, probably by suicide following a failed business venture, of his father; the wooing of a childhood sweetheart who has returned to the place of their childhood, and the consequences of the narrator killing her brother in a duel. The killing takes place "offstage" - the last section gives the narrator's reaction to the death after he has fled abroad, reports the death of Maud, and reveals his decision to go to war in the Crimea, partly to hide from his crime and partly to seek redemption. There is general agreement among critics that the narrator is unhinged by the death of his father and that much of the poem reflects psychosis and obsession. There are also sections which hark back to the emotions of *"In Memoriam"*, particularly when reflecting on the power of Love. The central story is intertwined with reflections on the new theories on evolution and the meaning of life in a world of scientific discovery, on the morality of war, and the role of religion.

I.xi – "O let the solid ground"

This section follows the narrator's re-meeting with Maud, whom he has not seen since they were children, and the beginning of his plan to woo her for his own. He has seen her pass in her carriage and at first thinks her cold, haughty and disdainful. However, a chance meeting in the village and in the church, reveals a softer side and she clearly remembers their childhood and seems friendly towards him. He is encouraged to pursue her. A complication is her brother's dislike of him and the arrival of a friend, a man newly-rich, whom the narrator believes has come in search of Maud as a bride.

Maud is written in a variety of metre, reflecting the mood swings of the narrator. **I.xi** is written in *iambic trimetre* - a jaunty metre of three stressed beats, and has a regular rhyme scheme of *ababcdc*. This may seem at odds with the subject matter, which is a reflection on the supremacy of Love in a life fulfilled. However, given its position in the whole poem, it can be seen as summing up the action that has gone before with a note of determination to pursue his goal of winning Maud's love, whatever the obstacles in his path and a fervent hope that he will not die before he achieves his goal. It also harks back to Canto 27 of "*In Memoriam*", where Tennyson seeks some form of reconciliation after his loss of Hallam:

I hold it true, whate'er befall;
I feel it when I sorrow most;
'Tis better to have loved and lost
Than never to have loved at all.

The poem is notable for the relative absence of Tennyson's usual poetic techniques, although the alliterated "*f*" in the first stanza, the repetition of phrases but with changed word order, and the regular rhyme scheme, keep it tightly structured and deceptively simple. It appears to be written in a simple vernacular, except for the repeated "*quite*" in the second stanza that breaks the rhythm, emphasising the poet's fervent desire to find love.

I
O let the solid ground
Not fail beneath my feet
Before my life has found
What some have found so sweet;
Then let come what come may,
What matter if I go mad,
I shall have had my day.

In the opening *quatrain,* the poet expresses his hope that he will not die before he finds love - the sweetness that others have found. Death is likened to the dissolving of the world. Plunging him into an abyss. Even if he goes mad later (and it is disturbing that he sees this as a possibility, given the tone of the poem as a whole, with its increasing paranoia), he will at least have experienced the emotion. The echo of the expression "*even a dog has its day*" is, again, a suggestion that all is not well with this man.

II
Let the sweet heavens endure,
Not close and darken above me
Before I am quite quite sure
That there is one to love me;
Then let come what come may
To a life that has been so sad,
I shall have had my day.

The next stanza recaps the idea, this time with a vision of death as if the sky above is darkening, suggesting internment in a grave. This is in opposition to the first stanza, where death was portrayed as the falling away of the ground. It is as if he is poised between the two on a knife edge – a *liminal space*. His need for reassurance about the presence of someone who loves him is conveyed by the repeated "*quite*", as if he finds it difficult to believe it himself. The narrator expresses the belief that even a short time secure in the love of another is better than no time at all, remaining alone. It is love of another which gives meaning to the world.

I.xviii – "I have led her home..."

This canto is similar to the first in the absence of the decoration often expected of Tennyson. It has a loose, conversational rhythm, irregular rhyme scheme - although there is rhyme throughout - and stanzas of varying length. There is much repetition and rephrasing of ideas and images. This structure, and the conversational *syntax*[8], seems to reflect the narrator's thought processes as he switches from Maud to reflections on the nature of Life, Love and Death, and back to Maud. It may reflect the chaotic, even psychotic, mind-set of the narrator that some critics have commented on. The narrator also uses a wealth of allusion to the Bible, in particular, as he seeks for images to define his beloved.

The narrator has taken advantage of Maud's brother's absence in town to declare his love to her in the garden where they meet. She seems to reciprocate. However, there is something in his actions of lurking in the garden that we might see as *"stalking"*. She seems unaware of his presence. This canto idolises the girl and reflects on the transcendence of Love over Death and how Love can bring meaning into the world.

I
I have led her home, my love, my only friend,
There is none like her, none.
And never yet so warmly ran my blood
And sweetly, on and on
Calming itself to the long-wished-for end,
Full to the banks, close on the promised good.

---

[8] *Syntax* is the order in which words are placed in a grammatical sentence.

"*Home*" refers to himself; he has brought her to where he believes she should be - with him. He likens his blood, his passion, to a river, almost overflowing its banks, running full to the sea - the "*long-wished-for end*", which is reciprocated love.

II
None like her, none.
Just now the dry-tongued laurels' pattering talk
Seem'd her light foot along the garden walk,
And shook my heart to think she comes once more;
But even then I heard her close the door,
The gates of Heaven are closed, and she is gone.

The repetition in the first line emphasises his passion. The personification of the laurels is typical Tennyson (see also comments on *"In Memoriam"*). It hints at the chattering tongues of others, as if he is aware that this love is illicit - or at least, not exactly being encouraged by her brother. He is excited that the sound might have been her footsteps, but disappointed when he hears the door slam and realises she has gone into the house. In likening the door of her house to "*Heaven*" he transitions to a comparison of Maud with Eve, in the next stanza.

The whole of the next two stanzas are addressed to a spreading Cedar of Lebanon - a tree with wide-spreading branches which can grow to an immense size - under which the narrator is lying and where he seems to be spending the night. The *syntax* is confusing. The main clause starts as a question, but there is no question mark and the subordinate clauses, which describe the tree and its location, make up most of the stanzas. So, the main clause is: "*O, art thou sighing for Lebanon...Dark Cedar (?)*".

III
There is none like her, none.
Nor will be when our summers have deceased.
O, art thou sighing for Lebanon

In the long breeze that streams to thy delicious East,
Sighing for Lebanon,
Dark cedar, tho' thy limbs have here increased,
Upon a pastoral slope as fair,
And looking to the South, and fed
With honeyed rain and delicate air,
And haunted by the starry head
Of her whose gentle will has changed my fate,
And made my life a perfumed altar-frame;
And over whom thy darkness must have spread
With such delight as theirs of old, thy great
Forefathers of the thornless garden, there
Shadowing the snow-limbed Eve from whom she came.

The narrator is asking the tree if it is longing for its homeland, when it seems to be *"sighing"* as the breeze blows through it, even though it has grown here in southern England where the air and rain is just as sweet as in Lebanon, because (by inference) Maud lives here (the "*starry head*"). The "*perfumed altar-frame*" suggests that he is going to spend his life in devotion to her from now on. He is sure that the tree must have been as happy to spread its branches over Maud as its ancestors were to spread theirs over Eve in the Garden of Eden, and makes a direct link between "*snow-limbed Eve*" and Maud, who is of course a *"daughter of Eve"*. Note the economy of the phrase "*thornless garden*" to describe Eden. Before the Fall, of course, the plants had no thorns, and all was peaceful and harmless. This is reminiscent of John Milton's phrase "*faded roses*" which is the first reference to death in his epic poem "*Paradise Lost*", where Adam brings back a bouquet to Eve and sees that she has eaten of the Tree of Knowledge:

"*From his slack hand the Garland wreath'd for Eve*
*Down drop'd, and all the **faded Roses** shed:*"

In those two words, all the horror and sorrow of the Fall is encapsulated.

IV
Here will I lie, while these long branches sway,
And you fair stars that crown a happy day
Go in and out as if at merry play,
Who am no more so all forlorn,
As when it seemed far better to be born
To labour and the mattock-hardened hand
Than nursed at ease and brought to understand
A sad astrology, the boundless plan
That makes you tyrants in your iron skies,
Innumerable, pitiless, passionless eyes,
Cold fires, yet with power to burn and brand
His nothingness into man.

Now that he knows that Maud reciprocates his love, the narrator can look upon the world more positively. He can lie under the tree, looking up at stars that now twinkle merrily, as if to celebrate this happy day. When he was *"forlorn"*, he had wondered whether it would have been better to have been brought up without an education, as a working man with hands hardened by manual labour, rather than be educated and learn that the stars and the universe ("*sad astrology*") were indifferent to Man and these "*cold fires*" (*oxymoron*[9]) merely emphasised Man's ("His") insignificance. The imagery here is of the new technology – furnaces to smelt iron – and recalls William Blake's poem *"Tyger, tyger"* with the lines:

---

[9] Two words juxtaposed which appear to contradict one another, as in *"bitter sweet"*. The stars look like little fires, but give no heat. Shakespeare littered *"Romeo and Juliet"* with *oxymorons* to underpin the theme of two opposites uniting.

What the hammer? what the chain,
In what furnace was thy brain?

This is a controversial point to make in Victorian times - the universe is the work of God and should reflect his Creation. This is indicative of the narrator's state of mind - but also a recurring theme in Tennyson's poetry, which questions the nature of faith and God.

V
But now shine on, and what care I,
Who in this stormy gulf have found a pearl
The countercharm of space and hollow sky,
And do accept my madness, and would die
To save from some slight shame one simple girl.

He instructs the stars to *"shine on"* as he can choose to ignore their nihilistic message now he has Maud (*"a pearl"*, precious and a symbol of purity) to live for and protect, which gives meaning to the world. *"simple girl"* means uncomplicated, innocent and natural.

VI
Would die; for sullen-seeming Death may give
More life to Love than is or ever was
In our low world, where yet 'tis sweet to live.
Let no one ask me how it came to pass;
It seems that I am happy, that to me
A livelier emerald twinkles in the grass,
A purer sapphire melts into the sea.

The narrator is now not afraid to die in the service of Maud; indeed, he suggests that the possibility of Death makes Love, and hence life, even sweeter. It is a mystery how it happened, but it brightens the whole world, the green of grass and the blue of the sea. These images are equated with Maud elsewhere - her feet in the grass and the blue of her eyes.

VII
Not die; but live a life of truest breath,
And teach true life to fight with mortal wrongs.
Oh, why should Love, like men in drinking-songs,
Spice his fair banquet with the dust of death?

He does not want to dwell on Death, but live his life fully and justly. He is prepared to fight for what he now believes in and dismiss fears of death. *"Spice"* here means to be aware that in the midst of life, we are in death, as it says in the Bible. The *"drinking-songs"* refer to songs sung before going into battle - there is a similar reference to men singing and drinking in Tennyson's great poem "*Ulysses*".

Make answer, Maud my bliss,
Maud made my Maud by that long loving kiss,
Life of my life, wilt thou not answer this?
"The dusky strand of Death inwoven here
With dear Love's tie, makes love himself more dear."

It is clear from this stanza that the two have exchanged kisses, which has convinced him of her love for him and that she is now "*his*". He seems to be urging her to commit to more - a very improper suggestion to make to a young Victorian girl who is under the protection of her family, possibly betrothed to another, and only seventeen! His argument is again that the presence of Death makes Love even sweeter.

VIII
Is that enchanted moan only the swell
Of the long waves that roll in yonder bay?
And hark the clock within, the silver knell
Of twelve sweet hours that past in bridal white,
And die to live, long as my pulses play;
But now by this my love has closed her sight
And given false death her hand, and stol'n away
To dreamful wastes where footless fancies dwell
Among the fragments of the golden day.
May nothing there her maiden grace affright!

The "*enchanted moan*" has sexual connotations and he goes on to refer to "*bridal white*" - her virginity - which has already wasted "*twelve sweet hours*". He refers to the clock chiming as a "*knell*", which is the tolling of a bell at a death. Rather, these sweet hours should have been spent making love, in response to the passion in his blood - his "*pulses*". The oxymoronic "*die to live*" is a pun, as used in Shakespeare, on orgasm. However, alas for him, it is late and Maud has gone to sleep and is dreaming, still innocent. He says farewell to the sleeping Maud, who has retained her virginity - her "*maiden grace*" - at least for now!

Dear heart, I feel with thee the drowsy spell.
My bride to be, my evermore delight,
My own heart's heart, my ownest own, farewell;
It is but for a little space I go:

The intensity of his passion is evident in the repetition and rephrasing, *"heart's heart/ownest own"*, as he struggles to articulate his desire. The idea of possessing her is also present in the repeated *"My"*. But he too is becoming sleepy, and decides to leave, or maybe sleep, for *"a little space"*.

And ye meanwhile far over moor and fell
Beat to the noiseless music of the night!
Has our whole earth gone nearer to the glow
Of your soft splendour that you look so bright?
I have climbed nearer out of lonely Hell.
Beat, happy stars, timing with things below,
Beat with my heart more blest than heart can tell.
Blest, but for some dark undercurrent woe
That seems to draw—but it shall not be so:

Let all be well, be well.

The *"ye"* could be addressed to Maud, but it is more likely to be to the stars, which he had seen as *"pitiless"*, but which now he believes are in tune with the world below them and which beat in time to the "music of the spheres" ("*the noiseless music*") which was a classical, philosophical concept about the harmony of proportions between the celestial bodies. He wonders whether the earth itself has moved nearer to them, as they look so bright. Certainly, he feels that he has come nearer to them, now his love has dispelled his loneliness, and, perhaps, the sorrow of his father's death. He and the stars (and Maud) are united in a joyous unity of the soul.

There is a momentary twinge of doubt that everything is going to end happily-ever-after, in the "*dark undercurrent of woe*" and the hyphenated break in the next line, but he rallies and prays that all will be well with his love and their life together.

(Spoiler alert: He is going to be bitterly disappointed.)

I. xxii – "Come into the garden, Maud"

This was possibly the most popular of the cantos among the general public, as it was made into a "parlour song" as early as 1857. To hear it sung rather well by a Professor of Musicology at Leeds, go to www.songsofthevictorians.com/index.html#songs. In the same archive, he has written an article with some interesting insights about the match of the music to the words. You want the setting by Balfe, not Sullivan.

The poem is remarkable for its sensuality. Gone is the colloquial style, the plain, unadorned language. This is Tennyson pulling out all the stops with passionate intensity, in spite of its rigid structure. It is written in *"common metre*[10]*"* - alternating lines of *iambic tetrametre* and *iambic trimetre* (four beats/three beats in a line) with a regular *ababab* rhyming scheme. This is predominantly sustained over eleven stanzas, showing Tennyson's technical mastery. Within this tight structure, he weaves a highly sensuous and erotic description of the garden and Maud, as well as conveying the obsessive nature of the narrator's passion.

The arrangement of the lines, with the alternate indenting, is a typographical convention of no significance other than to indicate the change in metric beat. The same can be said of the capitalisation of words at the beginnings of lines. Where a word is capitalised deliberately, it is often evident from similar usage elsewhere in the text, or by literary convention, as in the personification of the virtues, such as Love, Faith, Hope.

At this point in the long poem, the intentions of the brother's friend towards Maud are becoming clear and the brother is supporting his claim. He holds a party to which the would-be

---

[10] *"common metre"* is similar to *"ballad metre"* in the alternation of 4 and 3 beat lines. *Ballads* tend to be narrative and may have a looser rhyme scheme. I have used the word *"common metre"* unless the poem is also clearly a ballad.

bridegroom is invited - but our Narrator is not. The narrator stands in the garden as dawn breaks, waiting for Maud to keep her promise to visit him after the party.

i
Come into the garden. Maud,
For the black bat, night, has flown.
Come into the garden, Maud,
I am here at the gate alone;
And the woodbine spices are wafted abroad,
And the musk of the rose is blown.

The repeated entreaty sets the tone of longing which characterises the canto. The personification of "*night*" as the alliterative "*black bat*" adds to the description of the scene (bats fly at night) but also conveys that night is over, flown away. Both "*woodbine*" (honeysuckle) and roses have strong scents which are particularly noticeable at night. "*Blown*" here has the double meaning of "*blown by the wind*", as in "*wafted*", and finished - roses are described as "*blown*" when they are dropping their petals. So, we have in this first stanza a suggestion of an ending - although the narrator is waiting expectantly.

ii
For a breeze of morning moves,
    And the planet of Love is on high,
Beginning to faint in the light that she loves
    On a bed of daffodil sky,
To faint in the light of the sun she loves,
    To faint in his light, and to die.

The coming of dawn is heralded by Venus, the "*planet of Love*", named after the Roman goddess, being seen in the sky, but her light fading as the sun comes up. The image of Venus lying on a yellow bed fainting as the sun god Apollo arrives is erotic - notice the sun is personified as "*his light*", making this an overtly sexual reference. The Victorians are characterised as being prudish about sex, at least in public. They were, in fact, highly sexualised, as a glance at their paintings would reveal! Overt sexuality was made "acceptable" by placing nudity in a classical, biblical or mythological context. Paintings of domestic scenes also dealt with sexual politics, such as infidelity, promiscuity or betrayal, but in these the message was often embedded in visual imagery, such as the types of flowers, the light or objects in the background. Suppressed sexual desire is a central theme in the poetry and novels of the Brontes.

iii
All night have the roses heard
    The flute, violin, bassoon;
All night has the casement jessamine stirred
    To the dancers dancing in tune;
Till a silence fell with the waking bird,
    And a hush with the setting moon.

The narrator has been listening to the sounds of music from the party all night, from his hiding place in the garden, and he fancifully imagines the flowers to have been doing the same. "*Jessamine*" is jasmine - another highly scented flower which symbolises *attachment. (See below for a more detailed explanation of the "language of flowers".)* At dawn, the party breaks up. Notice the continual use of noun phrases - "*waking bird*", "*setting moon*" to paint a detailed picture in a few words.

iv
I said to the lily, 'There is but one
    With whom she has heart to be gay.
When will the dancers leave her alone?
    She is weary of dance and play.'
Now half to the setting moon are gone,
    And half to the rising day;
Low on the sand and loud on the stone
    The last wheel echoes away.

The narrator now addresses his flowery companions showing his impatience with Maud's absence - and his self-absorbed assumption that she would rather be with him than partying. The party is breaking up, with the guests departing their various ways, some east, some west, in their carriages, whose wheels make a quiet sound over soft ground, but are loud on cobbles or stone. Notice the *alliterated* "l" sounds on "*low/loud/last/wheel*" which highlights the *parallelism*[11] as the guests depart in different ways. These few stanzas paint a fascinating portrait of how Victorian society entertained.

v
I said to the rose, 'The brief night goes
    In babble and revel and wine.
O young lord-lover, what sighs are those,
    For one that will never be thine?
But mine, but mine,' so I sware to the rose,
    'For ever and ever, mine.'

The narrator shows his contempt for the party in the world "*babble*" and for the "*lord-lover*" who has come to woo Maud in that *portmanteau* word. He despises him, not only because he presumes to win Maud's love, but because of his status - what was called "*noveau riche*" - people whose money was acquired through trade and not land. The *lord-lover*'s father was in mining. The "*lord*" is ironic. The repeated "*mine*" shows the narrator's growing obsession - and of course, could be a deranged echo of the *lord*'s trade.

vi
And the soul of the rose went into my blood,
    As the music clashed in the hall;
And long by the garden lake I stood,
    For I heard your rivulet fall
From the lake to the meadow and on to the wood,

---

[11] *Parallelism* is the use of similar grammatical structures to link ideas.

Our wood, that is dearer than all;

He is shaken with passion as he listens to the music of the party. It *"clashes"* as it is not a sound that he associates with Maud. The *"rivulet"* that he hears is a cascade running through the grounds of the Hall, from the lake through a meadow and into the wood where they used to meet, a natural sound he contrasts with the noise of the party. The rivulet is THEIR sound.

vii
From the meadow your walks have left so sweet
  That whenever a March-wind sighs
He sets the jewel-print of your feet
  In violets blue as your eyes,
To the woody hollows in which we meet
  And the valleys of Paradise.

The Victorian's had a highly developed "language of love" through flowers. It was a way of signalling one's feelings about another without speaking. So, *"forget-me-not"*, a small, blue flower, meant just that. *Roses* are the traditional flower of *love* and *passion* and have featured in poetry as such since Chaucer in the 14th century at least. A contemporary, and charming, book on the subject, by Kate Greenaway, can be found at https://archive.org/details/languageofflower00gree. Click on the pages to turn them. This tradition was given a recent boost when Kate Middleton, the Duchess of Cambridge, chose flowers with specific meanings for her bridal bouquet.

He traces the course of the rivulet, imagining Maud walking there and the earthresponding by growing violets (*faithfulness*) where she steps. This is another common conceit used by poets and can be found also in William Congreve's "*Where'er You Walk*" (18th century), made famous by Handel in his oratorio *Semele*:

Where'er you tread
The Blushing flowers shall rise

*And all things flourish
Where'er you turn your eyes*

viii
*The slender acacia would not shake
        One long milk-bloom on the tree;
The white lake-blossom fell into the lake
        As the pimpernel dozed on the lea;
But the rose was awake all night for your sake,
        Knowing your promise to me;
The lilies and roses were all awake,
        They sighed for the dawn and thee.*

It appears that the acacia (*friendship* - too cold?) by the lake, and the scarlet pimpernel (*change; assignation*) nearby do not react to her passing, as the lake is not a place special to them - unlike the roses and lilies (*purity; sweetness*) in the garden.

ix
*Queen rose of the rosebud garden of girls,
        Come hither, the dances are done,
In gloss of satin and glimmer of pearls,
        Queen lily and rose in one;
Shine out, little head, sunning over with curls,
        To the flowers, and be their sun.*

The language here is a combination of passion and purity - his passion, her purity, although he, of course, hopes for the passion to be reciprocated. Although Maud's appearance is idealised, we do learn from these stanzas that she has blonde, curly hair and blue eyes. She is, in fact, quite vividly depicted in the poem as a whole (see *Canto I.ii*) where we learn that she has a full bottom lip and a slightly curved nose! Maud was modelled on Charlotte Rosa Baring who lived near Tennyson in Spilsby in Lincolnshire and the garden is the garden of her house.

x
There has fallen a splendid tear
　　From the passion-flower at the gate.
She is coming, my dove, my dear;
　　She is coming, my life, my fate;
The red rose cries, 'She is near, she is near;'
　　And the white rose weeps, 'She is late;'
The larkspur listens, 'I hear, I hear;'
　　And the lily whispers, 'I wait.'

The narrator's growing frustration at Maud's tardiness is echoed by the flowers all around him. The passion-flower (*religion and belief*) is a plant long associated with Christ's passion, as the flowers are made up in parts of three and five - the Trinity and the five wounds - head, hands, feet and side. This heightens the spiritual fervour he is feeling. The red rose is passionate in its conviction of her arrival, while the white rose ("*I am worthy*") cries as she continues to deny him; the larkspur (*haughtiness*) hears him, but does not respond. The repetition also reflects his increasing impatience – as does the increased use of *iambic trimetre* in the next stanza, quickening the pace.

xii
She is coming, my own, my sweet,
　　Were it ever so airy a tread,
My heart would hear her and beat,
　　Were it earth in an earthy bed;
My dust would hear her and beat,
　　Had I lain for a century dead;
Would start and tremble under her feet,
　　And blossom in purple and red.

The narrator reaffirms his belief that she will come to him and that, however lightly she were to walk, he would hear her and respond with all his being - even if he were dead in the ground beneath her feet. This idea is developed and he imagines himself as "*dust*" (from whence man came - as in "*dust to dust, ashes to ashes"* in the burial service) and that Maud has the power to resurrect him - again, a Christ-like image. Like Lazarus, he will rise from the dead. The final line reinforces the flower imagery that has run throughout the poem - his (brown, dead) *"dust"* will regrow and bloom in the colours of the roses that surround him, like his passion, as he waits.

Some critics interpret the final line as an image of violence. Given the flower imagery that precedes it, I am not convinced that this interpretation is supportable. A vivid and extreme evocation of a man's consuming passion, certainly.

This canto ends the second section of the whole poem. We are left wondering if Maud heeded his entreaty to *"Come into the garden"* or whether she was seduced by the music and dancing and remained at the party.

II.iv – "O that 'twere possible"

There is a break in the narrative between sections I and II. We left the narrator waiting for Maud in the garden. The opening of Part II makes it clear that something unfortunate has happened. Canto 1 of Part II opens:

I
"The fault was mine, the fault was mine, - "
Why am I sitting here so stunned and still,
Plucking the harmless wildflower on the hill?
It is this guilty hand!

Maud did meet with the narrator in the garden - but as soon as she arrives, they are discovered by the brother and the "*babe-faced lord*". A row ensues and the brother strikes the narrator and challenges him to a duel. In the duel, the narrator kills the brother. Dying, the brother claims "*the fault was mine*" and urges him to flee. The narrator flees to Brittany, from where he recalls and regrets his action, in spite of being absolved from blame by the brother. Soon after he arrives, he hears that Maud, too, has died - presumably from grief. This canto comes just after he has heard the news.

The canto is written in a fairly regular *common* metre of *iambic tetrametre* and *iambic trimetre* with an irregular rhyme scheme. The poem is propelled forward by the use of *enjambment*, which gives the whole canto, although reflective in subject matter, an underlying urgency, reflecting the pain of his loss - and also his desperation. He is a "murderer", he lives in self-imposed exile and his beloved is dead. This is not a happy situation.

i
O that 'twere possible
After long grief and pain
To find the arms of my true love
Round me once again!

There is a clear echo here of an anonymous 16th century poem called *"The Lover in Winter Plaineth for the Spring"* which begins:

O Western wind, when wilt thou blow
That the small rain down can rain?
Christ, that my love were in my arms
And I in my bed again!

The exclamatory tone continues in the third stanza - "*Ah, Christ...*" as he recalls his secret meetings with Maud:

ii
When I was wont to meet her
In the silent woody places
By the home that gave me birth,
We stood tranced in long embraces
Mixt with kisses sweeter sweeter
Than anything on earth.

He recalls their clandestine meetings where they would kiss, made even more poignant now that he is exiled from the place of his *"birth"*. Note the characteristic repetition of *"sweeter sweeter"* for emphasis.

iii
A shadow flits before me,
Not thou, but like to thee:
Ah Christ, that it were possible
For one short hour to see

The souls we loved, that they might tell us
What and where they be.

He imagines an image of Maud and wishes that she (and other dead people) could tell him the mysteries of the afterlife. This is a recurring theme in Tennyson - curiosity about what happens when we die, whether souls meet again, the power of memory to recapture the dead and the possibility of communion between them - no doubt engendered by the death of Hallam. Victorians, although still adhering to the established Church, were shaken by the findings of Darwin and others that called into question the absolute authority of the Bible and this extended to questioning the existence of an afterlife. It was an age in which Spiritualism - attempts to contact the dead "on the other side" – became very popular.

iv
It leads me forth at evening,
It lightly winds and steals
In a cold white robe before me,
When all my spirit reels
At the shouts, the leagues of lights,
And the roaring of the wheels.

He contrasts the unearthly vision of Maud, cold, pale and silent, with the clamour of the living world around him - a world which has lost its meaning, being reduced to light and noise. The use of enjambment at *"steals/in" "reels/At"* leads us through the stanza.

v
Half the night I waste in sighs,
Half in dreams I sorrow after
The delight of early skies;
In a wakeful doze I sorrow

For the hand, the lips, the eyes,
For the meeting of the morrow,
The delight of happy laughter,
The delight of low replies.

He recalls the pleasures of his meetings with Maud, which he dreams about at night. Notice the focus on the physical, which is similar to that expressed in *"In Memoriam",* and the use of repetition for emphasis.

vi
'Tis a morning pure and sweet,
And a dewy splendour falls
On the little flower that clings
To the turrets and the walls;
'Tis a morning pure and sweet,
And the light and shadow fleet;
She is walking in the meadow,
And the woodland echo rings;
In a moment we shall meet;
She is singing in the meadow,
And the rivulet at her feet
Ripples on in light and shadow
To the ballad that she sings.

Tennyson has written about "*splendour*" (glowing light) elsewhere: "*The splendour falls on castle walls.*" (*The Princess*). It is used to contrast the light of the living world with the darkness of death. His dream takes on a more vivid reality - note the opening in the present tense: "*Tis*" – it "***is***", and "*She **is** walking...*" The images of Maud are firmly lodged in the real world, which is described in minute detail - *little flower that clings/To the turrets...*" In the language of flowers, this would signify *constancy* and if we take Maud herself as "*the little flower*" then we have an image of her clinging on to life, and by inference, the narrator. There is a terrible poignancy in the vivid image of his Maud coming towards him in the repeated: "*She is walking...*", "*She is singing...*"

vii
Do I hear her sing as of old,
My bird with the shining head,
My own dove with the tender eye?
But there rings on a sudden a passionate cry,
There is some one dying or dead,
And a sullen thunder is roll'd;
For a tumult shakes the city,
And I wake, my dream is fled;
In the shuddering dawn, behold,
Without knowledge, without pity,
By the curtains of my bed
That abiding phantom cold.

viii
Get thee hence, nor come again,
Mix not memory with doubt,
Pass, thou deathlike type of pain,
Pass and cease to move about!
'Tis the blot upon the brain
That will show itself without.

The narrator awakes from his dream as he hears her cry out at the death of her brother. Her sweet image is replaced with one of horror - notice the *hypallage* (*transferred epithet*) in "*shuddering dawn*" – it is he who is shuddering, but he attributes the feeling to the dawn. Who or what this "*abiding phantom*" is, is unclear. It may be Death itself or Guilt or the image of the dead brother. Whichever, it is sufficiently unnerving to drive the narrator out of his room and into the streets. The tone changes from blissful reminiscence to pushing away horrid images - note the commands "*Get*", the repeated "*Pass*" – and he fears that his inner torment will show on the outside.

ix
Then I rise, the eave-drops fall,
And the yellow vapours choke
The great city sounding wide;
The day comes, a dull red ball
Wrapt in drifts of lurid smoke
On the misty river-tide.

x
Thro' the hubbub of the market
I steal, a wasted frame;
It crosses here, it crosses there,
Thro' all that crowd confused and loud,
The shadow still the same;
And on my heavy eyelids
My anguish hangs like shame.

The narrator goes out into the city. Tennyson uses *pathetic fallacy* in his description of the city to mirror the narrator's state of mind - dark, foggy, pestilent, shrouded, confused, where the former "*splendour*" of light in his dream has given way to the reality of "*a dull red ball*". He is isolated in his guilt and shame from the everyday life of the people around him, but the "*phantom*" or "*shadow*" is always with him – it "*crosses here*" and "*there*".

xi
Alas for her that met me,
That heard me softly call,
Came glimmering thro' the laurels

At the quiet evenfall,
In the garden by the turrets
Of the old manorial hall.

The narrator feels guilt also for Maud's death as he recalls their meetings. There is a blending of the past, living girl approaching him and the dead spirit of his dreams in the word "*glimmering*", as if she was/is a being of light. Note how the stanzas move seamlessly between his two states - the idyllic, remembered past, and his harsh reality.

xii
Would the happy spirit descend
From the realms of light and song,
In the chamber or the street,
As she looks among the blest,
Should I fear to greet my friend
Or to say "Forgive the wrong,"
Or to ask her, "Take me, sweet,
To the regions of thy rest"?

The first word "*Would*" means "*Were ... to*", so "*Were the happy spirit to descend...*" He wonders what he would do were she to come down from heaven in reality. Would he be too wracked with guilt to talk to her, or would he ask forgiveness, or would he ask her to take him with her up to heaven?

xiii
But the broad light glares and beats,
And the shadow flits and fleets
And will not let me be;
And I loathe the squares and streets,
And the faces that one meets,
Hearts with no love for me:

*Always I long to creep
Into some still cavern deep,
There to weep, and weep, and weep
My whole soul out to thee.*

In the light of day, there is to be no reconciliation between the living and the dead. The shadow of his past actions haunts him and isolates him from the living. Tennyson emphasises the narrator's feeling of alienation in the contrast between the world Maud inhabits in the previous stanza, *"light and song"*, by using *parallelism* with *"glares and beats"* and *"flits and fleets"*. He wishes only to go and hide in a cave where he can pour out his grief to Maud. The characteristic repeated *"and weep"*, suggests that all words and actions are now futile in the face of his overwhelming guilt and grief. The description of the streets with the blank faces of passers-by is reminiscent of *"In Memoriam – VII"*. It seems likely that this stanza is also a further homage to Hallam, as it shares much of the same imagery and overwhelming feelings of loss.

Introduction to the Brontes

To understand Charlotte and Emily Bronte's prose and poetry, you need to understand the circumstances of their short, and arguably tragic lives. The sisters had four siblings – two sisters who died, aged 10 and 12, of consumption (what we now know as tuberculosis, a chronic lung disease which was incurable at the time) while away at boarding school; a brother, Branwell, who eventually died of drink and drugs aged 31, and Anne, who also died of consumption aged 28, shortly after her brother's death. Emily died in the same year as Anne, aged 30. Charlotte, the only one to marry, died in childbirth in 1855, aged 39.

For much of their short lives they lived in relative isolation high on the Yorkshire Moors in the parsonage of the village of Haworth, where their father was the parson. The landscape of the Moors infuses their writings. Their mother died when they were very young and they were brought up by their aunt, who was a strict Methodist. Their lives were characterised by self-improvement, religiosity and study. Branwell was educated at home, but the four girls attended school for a time and, for the standards of the day, were well-read. In childhood, they were left to their own resources for entertainment and amused themselves by chronicling the events of two imaginary countries – Gondal and Angria – writing the stories and poems in tiny, handmade booklets. The young women hoped to make a living by teaching and were for a time governesses and tutors; Charlotte and Emily lived briefly in France learning French. However, their dreams of starting their own school in England came to nothing when Mr Bronte's eyesight began to fail and Branwell sank into despair, drugs and drink following a scandalous affair with the wife of his employer. Thereafter, they were largely confined to Haworth. There is an overview of Emily's and her sisters' lives at www.poetryfoundation.org/poems-and-poets/poets/detail/emily-bronte.

"The Visionary" – Emily and Charlotte Bronte

This poem is often assigned to Emily Bronte alone, although it is believed that Charlotte revised or rewrote the final two stanzas. Emily is variously described by biographers and critics as "spiritual" and "visionary", as well as highly imaginative. This poem clearly refers to a visitation by some kind of spiritual being; whether it is the Christian God, an emissary from Him in the form of an angel, a Presence outside formal religion or about the Creative Process, is harder to determine. It should perhaps be remembered, also, that although Emily appears to have never had any kind of romantic liaison with a man (or woman), she is the author of *Wuthering Heights* – a novel centred on one of literature's most iconic male characters, Heathcliff. The novel is full of passionate intensity, with a doomed love-affair at its heart. It might not be too fanciful to suggest that, while not exactly a metaphor for the visit of a lover, there is clear fusing of the spiritual and the physical in its evocation of the intense longing of The Visionary to be united with its Vision.

Emily and Charlotte Bronte's poems can be considered largely autobiographical in the sense that hers is the narrative voice – even if the poems are from the Gondal or Angria fantasies of their youth. In this poem, the poet is essentially The Visionary – there is no real reason to distinguish between the two.
There is a rather good analysis of this poem at www.yurtopic.com/education/books/visionary-analysis.html and on Emily Bronte at
www.victorianweb.org/authors/bronte/ebronte/wiseman1.html

The poem is written in *iambic hexametres*, also called *alexandrines* – six beats in a line – and has a regular *aabb* rhyme scheme. These long lines and regular rhythm give the poem a tone of quiet surety – a conviction that the longed-for Vision will come – whilst allowing Bronte to detail the contrast between indoors and out, and use half-lines to both sustain and vary the tempo and mood.

Silent is the house: all are laid asleep:
One alone looks out o'er the snow-wreaths deep,
Watching every cloud, dreading every breeze
That whirls the wildering drift, and bends the groaning trees.

The first line uses the *caesura* (the break in the middle of the line) to give two, reinforcing images of the scene indoors, where The Visionary awaits the coming of the Vision. She draws our view to look out on to the winter scene which, in contrast to the cosy interior, is wild and threatening – she is *"dreading"* the breeze as it may hinder the approach of the Vision. *"Wildering"* is the participle of *"to wilder"*, which means to lead astray; it is now archaic, although still used in the form of *"bewildered"*, meaning confused. The scene she describes is the wild Yorkshire moorland that loomed over the parsonage and to which Emily, particularly, was drawn, finding in it both inspiration and solace. There is a strong feeling of *place* in most of the Bronte's poems.

Cheerful is the hearth, soft the matted floor;
Not one shivering gust creeps through pane or door;
The little lamp burns straight, its rays shoot strong and far:
I trim it well, to be the wanderer's guiding-star.

The poet brings us back indoors for further contrast between indoors and out, again using the caesura to give us two, reinforcing, views of the interior. *"Shivering gust"* is hypallage (a *transferred epithet*). It is the watcher who would shiver in the cold air. This time, there is a more assertive tone in the words *"Not one"*, *"straight"*, *"shoot strong"* – nothing can penetrate this haven. She has slammed the door against the winter cold and against doubt. The lamp light, which is an oil-lamp, as she *"trims"* the wick, sends out a clear beam which the Vision can use to find the way, just as travellers used to navigate by the stars.

Frown, my haughty sire! chide, my angry dame!
Set your slaves to spy; threaten me with shame:
But neither sire nor dame nor prying serf shall know,
What angel nightly tracks that waste of frozen snow.

There is an abrupt shift in tone here (at the point where Charlotte is presumed to have taken over) to an angry rebuttal of the suggestion that what the Visionary is doing is foolish or, at least, not approved by the masters of the house (or her parents? It seems a little harsh, if so!) This raises the interesting question of the Visionary's status in this house – child? servant? adult daughter? It is not explicit. Again, she uses the half line to reinforce an idea signalled by the two imperatives – *"frown"* and *"chide"* – and the second line to detail their imagined reaction – which is to set their servants to spy on her, or expose her (as a fraud?). Both the words *"slave"* and *"serf"* are archaic (as are *"sire"* and *"dame"*) in this context and used for exaggeration, to give added emphasis to her contempt for their censure. The long third line brings the reader back to a calmer state of mind as she reasserts her unswerving conviction of the Vision's (*"angel"*) arrival.

It is arguable that the poet's anger is directed towards those members of Victorian society who were becoming increasingly sceptical of the existence of a God, as new scientific theories were published. The Visionary declares her steadfast faith in the face of this scepticism.
This stanza also brings the confusion, or merger, of a spiritual visitor with a physical one. The word *"shame"* seems a slightly odd charge against someone having a spiritual or religious vision – unless there is a prohibition against it of which the reader is not

made aware – but *shame* for sexual transgressions was expected from the transgressor. The *"angel"* (clearly a spiritual reference) *"tracks"* (leaves footprints) in the snow - a physical rather than spiritual manifestation. This melding of physical and spiritual continues in the next stanza.

What I love shall come like visitant of air,
Safe in secret power from lurking human snare;
What loves me, no word of mine shall e'er betray,
Though for faith unstained my life must forfeit pay.

We learn that the visitor is *"like"* air and has *"secret power"* that protects it from prying eyes and mere human traps, suggesting that it is spiritual. But this "thing" also *"loves"* her – is susceptible to human emotions, and is also a love that must be kept secret, even if keeping true to it costs her life. This suggests that the longed-for Vision is not unlike the visions of Saint Joan of Arc, the 15th century French martyr who died fighting for France – an intense spiritual experience which has manifest physical symptoms.

Burn, then, little lamp; glimmer straight and clear—
Hush! a rustling wing stirs, methinks, the air:
He for whom I wait, thus ever comes to me;
Strange Power! I trust thy might; trust thou my constancy.

The last stanza reaffirms her faith, as symbolised by the lamp, and heralds the arrival of the *"Strange Power"* in the form of an angel with *"rustling wing"*. She ends with a cry of affirmation – a belief in the power of the Vision and a desire that her faithful devotion be reciprocated.

"Grief" – Elizabeth Barrett Browning

A useful biography of EBB can be found at www.poetryfoundation.org/poems-and-poets/poets/detail/elizabeth-barrett-browning. It gives the probable context for this poem as being the death by drowning of EBB's brother, Edward. It was written during, or shortly after her return from, three years spent in Torquay where she had moved to try and improve her health; for much of her life, EBB was sickly and spent months/years largely confined to her room.

The poem is a *Petrarchan sonnet* - 14 lines of *iambic pentametre* with a regular rhyme scheme *abbaabba* (*octet*[12]) *cdecde* (*sestet*[13]). Petrarch was the prime exponent of the sonnet form in Italy in the 14th century but it was adopted in England by Shakespeare and others, although sometimes with a different rhyme scheme.

Sonnets are traditionally love poems, although modern sonnets can cover any kind of experience. They usually put forward some kind of argument or premise - an idea for discussion - in the *octet* which is answered or countered in the *sestet*, although in Shakespeare this "answer" can occur as late as the final two lines. This switch in the argument, or answer to the question, is called the *volta,* or *"turn".* You can find a good, more detailed, exploration of sonnet form, with ideas for writing your own, at www.poetryfoundation.org/resources/learning/articles/detail/70051.

The poem deals with the nature of Grief and contests the popular perception of grief being manifest through the "wailing and gnashing of teeth" - loud declarations of sorrow. In contrast, she experiences grief as a feeling of lifelessness, like being a statue.

---

[12] An *octet* is eight lines
[13] A *sestet* is six lines

I tell you, hopeless grief is passionless;

The reader is directly accosted by the poet's argument. She puts forward her premise bluntly, as if to reject any counter argument, which is that true grief is expressed without the outward shows of violent emotion.

That only men incredulous of despair,
Half-taught in anguish, through the midnight air
Beat upward to God's throne in loud access
Of shrieking and reproach.

In line 2, the "*I tell you*" is implied as in "(*I tell you) That only men ...*". She is addressing people (*men* is a gender-neutral form) who do not believe in, or have not experienced, despair, or have only a partial understanding ("*half-taught*") of the pain of sorrow, who take out their feelings on God with loud prayers and wailing.

Note how the strict rhyme scheme is softened by the use of enjambment between "*access/Of*" and the use of the *caesura* after *"reproach"* which sets up the line to similarly run into the next, keeping the whole sonnet moving forward.

*   Full desertness,*
In souls as countries, lieth silent-bare
Under the blanching, vertical eye-glare
Of the absolute heavens.

The soul experiencing true grief is as barren and lifeless as a desert, exposed to the pitiless sun – and the eye of God. The *volta* occurs at the *caesura,* after "*heavens",* where she now addresses men of true feeling ("*Deep-hearted man*") and expounds on her idea of what grief really feels like.

Deep-hearted man, express
Grief for thy dead in silence like to death—
Most like a monumental statue set
In everlasting watch and moveless woe
Till itself crumble to the dust beneath.

True grief is expressed in a death-like silence, like an ancient statue which sits motionless until it crumbles into dust. It can do nothing else, being lifeless.

Touch it; the marble eyelids are not wet:
If it could weep, it could arise and go.

The truth of her analogy is given in the final couplet. She urges (us) to *"Touch"* the statue, metaphorically the person silent and motionless in grief, and we will find that the eyes are dry. If they had the power to weep, then they would also have the power to move on and, by inference, leave the grief behind. However, the true griever cannot *"move on"*.

The image of a statue in a desert is similar to the sonnet "*Ozymandias*" by John Keats, published in 1818, which can be found www.poetryfoundation.org/resources/learning/core-poems/detail/46565 and which EBB would almost certainly have known.

From "Sonnets from the Portuguese" – XX1V –
Elizabeth Barrett Browning

The unlikely love-affair, and marriage, of Elizabeth Barrett and Robert Browning is one of the great love stories of the Victorian age. After her return from Torquay, Elizabeth was largely confined to the house, writing her poetry and letters. She published in journals and, in 1844, a two-volume collection of her poetry was published on both sides of the Atlantic, heralding her as one of the foremost poets of her day. The two volumes reached the house of Robert Browning, himself a published poet, but struggling to establish himself. The two began to write to each other, a correspondence, and courtship, which lasted for two years before they eloped in 1846 to escape the disapproval of Elizabeth's father. They moved to Italy, where they stayed until Elizabeth's death in 1861.

"*Sonnets from the Portuguese*" were written during the period of Robert's courtship and are love poems written about her experience of falling and being in love and often addressed to Robert himself – as in the "*Dear*" of this sonnet.

This is another *Petrarchan sonnet*. The *volta* again appears half-way through the 8th line, with a switch from the comparison of the world's ills to a pen-knife, rendered harmless by being closed and held in the hand of love, to a comparison of love to lilies that grow by God's grace.

Let the world's sharpness, like a clasping knife,
Shut in upon itself and do no harm
In this close hand of Love, now soft and warm,
And let us hear no sound of human strife
After the click of the shutting.

The central image is a comparison between the unpleasantness ("*sharpness*") of the world and a knife, specifically a knife that has a folding blade, like a pen-knife. She imagines the knife shutting, rendering it harmless, and being held in her hand – a hand that is itself a metaphor for Love. Once held shut in her hand, the knife can do no harm – the world with its ills cannot intrude upon the world of the Lovers. The use of the *onomatopoeic "click"* taken together with the caesura on *"shutting"* echoes the action of the clasp knife folding in.

Life to life –
I lean upon thee, Dear, without alarm,
And feel as safe as guarded by a charm
Against the stab of worldlings, who if rife
Are weak to injure.

The idea of the world being injurious is continued. However, supported by her lover, the poet feels safe, as if protected by magic against any harm that the world can do – however numerous the assailants might be; *"worldlings"* are people living in the world who, by inference, intend harm towards the lovers. You could substitute "muggles"!

Very whitely still
The lilies of our lives may reassure
Their blossoms from their roots, accessible
Alone to heavenly dews that drop not fewer,
Growing straight, out of man's reach, on the hill.
God only, who made us rich, can make us poor.

The sestet switches to a second image, this time of their Love. It is likened to white lilies, symbols of purity, which draw nourishment *"from their roots"*. These roots are watered from the heavens by God. They grow straight and tall on the hillside out of the reach of man, meaning that their love is sanctioned by God and cannot be sullied by other people. This is summarised in the final line – God gave them their love and only he can take it away.

The poem might be an oblique reference to her father's opposition to the courtship. A widower, he wanted to keep his children dependent on him. It may also be a riposte to those who thought the relationship odd – Elizabeth was six years older than Robert and at times, had doubts herself about marrying him as she was older and in such poor health. Here, it seems that these doubts are put aside in the reassurance of Robert's love for her and the strength this give the two of them together against the world.

"The Best Thing in the World" – Elizabeth Barrett Browning

This poem reminds me of the song from "*The Sound of Music*", a hugely popular musical, filmed in 1965, with lyrics and music by Rogers and Hammerstein. It shot Julie Andrews to stardom and the opening scene, with her twirling around on a mountainside singing "*The Hills are Alive...*" has passed into legend. "*Favorite Things*" starts:

Raindrops on roses and whiskers on kittens
Bright copper kettles and warm woollen mittens
Brown paper packages tied up with string
These are a few of my favorite things

and goes on to list a number of other "favorite things". You can listen to and read the song sung by Andrews at www.youtube.com/watch?v=kPfgGkyUzEk.

The anthology only gives the publication date of this poem (1862), which is after her death, so it is hard to place this in the chronology of her life. However, as there is a clear reference to Robert in the poem, we can assume it was written either during the period of her courtship or after her marriage.

The poem is deceptively simple. EBB was versed in a number of languages, including the Classics and Hebrew, and had read a vast amount of literature. She also had a religious upbringing and seems to have retained her faith throughout her life. It may sound simple, but it is built on literary and classical allusions. It is written in *iambic tetrametre* which gives it a light-hearted, bouncy rhythm that perhaps belies the seriousness of her message – which is supported by the scholarly references and a possible interpretation of the final line. However, it is not a sonnet – usually used for "serious" love poetry – so it may indeed be a playful *"diversion"* or *"divertimento"* poem. The line on *Love*, discussed below, certainly suggests a tone of whimsy.

What's the best thing in the world?

The poem starts with a rhetorical question, the direct address reminiscent of the opening of *"Grief"*. She then continues with two images, drawn from nature:

June-rose, by May-dew impearled;
Sweet south-wind, that means no rain;

This is *"Raindrops on roses"*, with the drops of dew likened to pearls. *"Impearled"* as a word goes back to Middle English, but is usually only found in poetry. Browning's language is usually vernacular rather than literary, so this may be a deliberate echo of John Milton in Book V of *"Paradise Lost"*:

Dewdrops which the sun
Impearls on every leaf and every flower

The link between *"dewdrops"* and *"pearls"* can also be found in Shakespeare:

I must go seek some dewdrops here,
And hang a pearl in every cowslip's ear.
            Midsummer Night's Dream

The south wind, or *sirocco*, is usually drier than others, as it travels overland from Africa.

Truth, not cruel to a friend;
Pleasure, not in haste to end;
Beauty, not self-decked and curled
Till its pride is over-plain;

Light, that never makes you wink;
Memory, that gives no pain;

EBB now personifies ideas from Greek mythology - Truth or *Aletheia*, which means not just "telling the Truth" but also being open and sincere, and two *Graces* or *Charites*. The *Charites* were the daughters of Zeus and Euronyme. They are often referred to as *"The Three Graces"* – *Beauty*, Charm and Joy (*Pleasure*). The actual number, and their attributes, varies. *Memory* or Greek *Mnemosyne*, was mother of the Muses.

EBB qualifies each by a descriptor of what she does NOT mean – *Truth* without hurtful bluntness; *Pleasure* which is not self-serving; *Beauty* which is natural and not adorned with make-up and elaborate hairstyles so that it becomes a form of pride; *Light* that is never so blinding as to make you shut your eyes; *Memory* that only recalls positive experiences.

The last attribute is *Love* – not one of the Greek *charites*, but a Christian virtue (as in Faith, Hope, *Charity* – usually modernised to *Love*). However, this *Love* is more secular:

*Love, when, **so**, you're loved again.*

Elizabeth is being playful. She means *Love* that is reciprocated – returned. And to demonstrate this, she breaks off - "*so*" - to kiss Robert. The "*so*" means "*like this*". Notice it is *italicised* in the anthology – I have boldened it here to show her deliberate choice of typography, which is presumably reproduced from her manuscript. (I cannot find the manuscript online to check). Even so, the punctuation, with the "*so*" separated by commas, suggests she is breaking her train of thought, as otherwise the line would have the same *syntax* as those preceding, viz:

Love, when you're loved again.

She ends as she began with a rhetorical question – and gives a somewhat ambiguous answer.

What's the best thing in the world?
--Something out of it, I think.

This last line can be variously interpreted. It could mean *"something out of the above list"* or *"something that can be taken out of the world"*, as in *"found in the world."* However, a further interpretation is that she is acknowledging that all of the items in her list are given by God – something literally *"out of it (the world)"*. Positive experiences, as those listed, can only be enjoyed by the grace of God. This is the same affirmation as at the end of "Sonnet XXIV": *"God only, who made us rich, can make us poor."*

"*Died...*" – Elizabeth Barrett Browning

I have searched and searched to try and find the subject of this poem - including looking in *The Times* archives. There are a few discussions online about it - but no conclusions. All we have is the date of death - "*On Sunday, 3rd of August*" - and, as the poem was published posthumously, (*Last Poems, 1862*), no date of composition. However, the dates can be narrowed down, as the poem is clearly addressed to her husband, Robert, as they seem to be having an argument about the merits of the dead person. This means there are only three possible dates - 1845 (before they were married, but during their courtship), 1851 and 1856, as these are the only years in which 3rd August fell on a Sunday, whilst they were together. (This comes courtesy of an - unresolved - online discussion). The person in question need not have been particularly famous - notices of death were, and are, commonly put in *The Times* personal columns. For many years, they were on the front page. Obituaries, as opposed to death notices, were usually written about more notable personalities.

The poem is written in five line stanzas of *iambic tetrametre* with a regular *abbaa* rhyme scheme. On first reading, this can seem rather trite and the tone of the whole somewhat flippant. However, the bantering tone of the first two stanzas soon gives way to a more serious reflection on the nature of fame, reputation and death and a scornful rejection of man's presumption in thinking that what we say about one another on earth can possibly matter in the face of death and God's judgement. The whole feels like one side of a conversation between two people who know each other well, are used to debate, and have something serious to say about a shared experience. This is a very different EBB from that of the sonnets. The tone is more authoritative and confident, more like "*Aurora Leigh*" her long narrative poem that addresses many social ills of the period.

The death seems to be unexpected - or, at least, the two seem to be in the middle of an on-going debate on the worthiness of the person's life, when they hear of his death through an obituary in the *"The Times"* newspaper.

I
What shall we add now? He is dead.
And I who praise and you who blame,
With wash of words across his name,
Find suddenly declared instead—
"On Sunday, third of August, dead".

The poem opens in the same direct, rhetorical style as the others in the selection and here she addresses her husband. Her opinion of the dead person is more positive than her husband's. Their debate is described in a metaphor – *"wash of words"* – which suggests not only that there have been a lot of them, but also that they have not had much effect, as in to "wash over". The bold notice of his death, which sounds as if it is lifted directly from the newspaper, designed to pull them (and us) up short (*"which stops"*), as if to underline the futility of their debate in the face of death.

II
Which stops the whole we talked to-day.
I quickened to a plausive glance
At his large general tolerance
By common people's narrow way,
Stopped short in praising. Dead, they say.

EBB seems to be recapping the point of her discussion. She recalls becoming animated (*"quickened"*) and praising the dead person for his liberality (*tolerance*), in contrast with the majority – the *"common people's narrow way"*. This could be political or social liberality, as EBB was an activist on many fronts. She wrote extensively about the plight of the poor in London, children in particular, even while she was living in Italy. Her two most famous poems on this are *"A Plea for the Ragged Schools of London"* (1854), published in a fund-raising pamphlet together with a poem by Robert Browning, *"The Twins"*, and *"The Cry of the Children"* (1842). However, her praises are *"stopped short"* by the death announcement.

III
And you, who had just put in a sort
Of cold deduction--"rather, large
Through weakness of the continent marge,
Than greatness of the thing contained"--
Broke off. Dead!--there, you stood restrained.

EBB now recaps for Robert what he had been saying, which was less fulsome in its praise of the man – in fact, rather *"cold"*. She quotes Robert's words, where he used a metaphor of a large object appearing bigger in a confined space. *"continent marge"* means the extent of the surrounding land and *"thing contained"* means what is inside the space. The liberality of the subject was only notable *because of* this contrast with the general population – made bigger than it really was by comparison. But Robert, too, breaks off from his argument when the news is received and is silenced.

IV
As if we had talked in following one
Up some long gallery. "Would you choose
An air like that? The gait is loose—
Or noble.' Sudden in the sun
An oubliette winks. Where is he? Gone.

EBB then uses a (rather odd) simile to elaborate on the effect of the sudden news. She imagines herself and Robert walking behind a person in a long, narrow room and commenting on the way they walk. But the discussion is made shockingly irrelevant because, suddenly, there is a *"wink"* in the light and some hole in space appears into which the man disappears – *"Gone"*. An *"oubliette"*, literally meaning *"forgotten"*, is a kind of dungeon which can only be accessed through a hole in the ceiling – effectively condemning the poor prisoner to indefinite incarceration.

V
Dead. Man's "I was' by God's "I am'—
All hero-worship comes to that.

EBB now moves on, still addressing Robert, to a more general reflection on the irrelevance of man's account of himself and others in their lives (*"I was"*) compared to the absolute judgement of God, the final arbiter (*"I am"*). The *"I am"* is a reference to *"I am Alpha and Omega, the beginning and the last"* from the Book of Revelations in the New Testament. *Alpha* (A) is the first and *Omega* (Ω) the last letter in the Greek alphabet, from which the English versions of the Book were translated.

High heart, high thought, high fame, as flat
As a gravestone. Bring your Jacet jam—
The epitaph's an epigram.

EBB shows the futility of their previous argument in the face of death with the scornful use of the repeated *"high"*, which is brought, literally, down to earth, by the use of the enjambment across the line from *"flat"* to *"As a gravestone"*. She then plays on the words *"He is dead"* or *"He lies here"* (*"iacet iam"* in Latin) declaring that these words are not just words written on his grave as a matter of fact (*epitaph*), but also a summary of all that can be said about him (*epigram*). An *epigram* is a short, usually witty, saying to sum someone up, so she is being ironic here. Oscar Wilde famously wrote *epigrams*, as in "*We are all in the gutter, but some of us are looking at the stars.*"

VI
Dead. There's an answer to arrest
All carping. Dust's his natural place?
He'll let the flies buzz round his face
And, though you slander, not protest?
--From such an one, exact the Best?

This stanza continues in the same mocking tone. She reiterates that the fact of Death is sufficient to stop anybody bad-mouthing the dead man (*carping*). The rhetorical questions that follow emphasise how little judgements made on him will matter to the dead man. If you slander him, by saying that he is so low or base as to be in the metaphorical "*Dust*", what does he care, and why should he *protest* as, being dead, he is not even bothered by having flies buzz around him? What can you expect to get from someone in his situation?

VII
Opinions gold or brass are null.
We chuck our flattery or abuse,
Called Caesar's due, as Charon's dues,
I' the teeth of some dead sage or fool,
To mend the grinning of a skull.

It doesn't matter what we think about people. We throw around (*chuck*, although sounding modern, was used to mean *throw* from the 16th century) our good or bad opinions about both wise (*sage*) or stupid (*fool*) people, as if it is our right and they deserve it.

"*Caesar's dues*" is a reference again to the Bible, where Jesus replies to a question about Jews paying taxes to the Romans – "*Render unto Caesar the things that are Caesar's; render unto God the things that are God's.*" We are, in fact, merely throwing them at the dead as if we could stave off inevitable death ourselves. *Charon's dues* are the coins paid to Charon, the ferryman who rowed the souls of the dead across the River Styx to Hades in Greek mythology. The "*grinning skull*" is a "*memento mori,*" or reminder of death, which originated in Roman times. You can read about it and see representations of them in paintings, which were very common throughout the medieval and early modern eras, www.en.wikipedia.org/wiki/Memento_mori.

The poem ends with a piece of advice to Robert, and more generally, the reader:

VIII
Be abstinent in praise and blame.
The man's still mortal, who stands first,
And mortal only, if last and worst.
Then slowly lift so frail a fame,
Or softly drop so poor a shame.

Resist the temptation to judge people – everyone is mortal, whether they are the very best or absolute worst. Instead, help people to become the best they can be (*slowly lift*) and don't be over-harsh (*softly drop*) on those who fail to live up to your high standards, as both good and bad qualities will not last beyond death.

This is a difficult poem to comprehend. There is considerable economy with words, with ideas compressed into small spaces, forced by the confines of the rhythm and rhyming schemes. The tone is both scornful and mocking, although there is a softening of the tone in the final two lines, through the use of the alliterative "*lift so frail a fame*", the *antithesis*[14] in "*slowly lift*" and "*softly drop*" and the merging of the conceptual - "*fame/shame*" – into the physical, as if it is a body that should be handled carefully.

---

[14] *antithesis* means balancing opposites – *on the one hand...on the other*

"My Last Duchess" – Robert Browning

This is the greatest poem in the whole selection, and possibly (probably) one of the greatest poems ever written. It is certainly the greatest *dramatic monologue* - the one against which all other poems in this form are judged. Browning is the master of this form, although not the only practitioner. Tennyson also wrote *dramatic monologues* which are among his best poems – *Ulysees* and *Tithonus*. *Maud,* which is discussed elsewhere in the blog, is also a *dramatic monologue*. A *dramatic monologue* is a poem where the poet takes on a *persona* - a character who is not himself - and speaks in his voice. However, that is not to say that the poet is entirely absent. The poet may refer to emotions, events or ideas which he has himself experienced, or be using the *persona* to debate topical questions of the day. The Victorian poets used the form to debate the position of women in society, sexual relationships and gender identity, the nature of work and finding purpose in life, religious doubt and societal ills, in their search to make sense of their lives in a world that was rapidly changing. The *dramatic monologue* allowed them the freedom to explore radical ideas without the fear of public censure. They were not always successful in the last - commentators of the day sometimes saw through the pretence and criticised them as scandalous.

Browning delighted in exploring the minds of socio- and psychopaths: *Porphyria's Lover* is a murderer; the woman in *The Laboratory* is planning to poison at least three of her rivals in love; the Duke has ordered a murder. Browning also wrote *dramatic monologues* based on Renaissance artists, as in *Fra Lippo Lippi* and *Andrea del Sarto*.

Poetry is an oral art form. It is the poet's voice - heard through the rhythm, the rhyme, *syntax* and punctuation, as well as the auditory poetic techniques - which lifts the words off the page and makes sense of them. To understand a *dramatic monologue*, you have to HEAR the voice. With the *dramatic monologue*, and

Browning's in particular, you have to be sensitive to what the *persona* is NOT saying, as much as to what he IS saying. We hear Browning's views on his subject, and his subject matter, in the gaps. The technique which he uses most to create the cadence of the voice of the *persona* and reveals what he is actually like, as opposed to the version of himself that he gives the listener, is *enjambment* - running the sense of a line onto the next (giving emphasis to the first words of the succeeding line) and *caesura* - breaking or stopping in the middle of the line.

The frequent use of these techniques not only reveals to us the true story behind the persona's version of it, but allows the poem to flow, uninterrupted, for 55 lines, whilst maintaining a regular rhyme scheme of *rhyming couplets* (*aabbccdd....*), which is a technical feat in itself. Added to that, it is written in *iambic pentametre.* And yet, read with sensitive attention to the flow of the sense in relation to the lines, both the regularity of the rhyme and the rhythm go all but unnoticed. And where they are noticeable, there is a very good reason for them to be so. I strongly advise you to listen to a recording of this work and you could do worse than listen to this dramatised reading by Julian Glover, at www.youtube.com/watch?v=i5AoZY6a_kE which is not very good quality, but captures the subtleties, as does this one by the late actor James Mason: www.youtube.com/watch?v=_ZbNrNE9q8g. Just ignore the painting which accompanies the last - it is Victorian, not Renaissance, which is when Browning's poem is set.

Browning's poem is based on the true story of the marriage between Alfonso, Duke of Ferrara and Lucrezia de 'Medici in the 16th century. The background can be found in Wiki here: https://en.wikipedia.org/wiki/My_Last_Duchess There is a wealth of material on the web about this poem, as it is one of the most anthologised and studied.

My Last Duchess
Ferrara

That's my last Duchess painted on the wall,
Looking as if she were alive. I call
That piece a wonder, now; Fra Pandolf's hands
Worked busily a day, and there she stands.

First, note the pun in the title. Does *"Last"* here mean final, as in *"the last one I will ever have?"* or *"The last one in a continuing line"*? The answer is given in the poem, but forms part of the intrigue of the opening. The title is repeated in the first line, but immediately given a sinister overtone: *"looking as if she were alive."* This could be a reference to it being a *life-like* painting – or is it a reference to something else? The pride the Duke takes in the painting is evident – *"a wonder"* - so maybe he is simply reflecting on the skill of Fra Pandolf, the painter. Notice how the pattern of *enjambment* and *caesura* is set up, making the regular rhyme-scheme all but unnoticeable.

Will't please you sit and look at her? I said
"Fra Pandolf" by design, for never read
Strangers like you that pictured countenance,
The depth and passion of its earnest glance,
But to myself they turned (since none puts by
The curtain I have drawn for you, but I)
And seemed as they would ask me, if they durst,
How such a glance came there; so, not the first
Are you to turn and ask thus.

It now becomes evident that the Duke is not talking to the reader, but to an unseen listener, although the effect is to put us, the reader, in that second person's place. And it also becomes clear that this is not the first time that the Duke has shown the picture to a visitor, and their reaction to the painting has been similar – amazement at the *"depth and passion of its earnest glance"* – and they all ask the same question – *"how such a glance came*

The regular *iambic* line gives way to a series of broken lines as the Duke reveals what he has done, conversationally. Browning uses a *spondee* to give sinister emphasis to the Duke's admittance of murder "Then all **smiles stopped**". The meaning of his introductory words, *"as if alive"*, repeated here and placed chillingly at the beginning of the line, are now clear. He has had her murdered on his orders.

Will't please you rise? We'll meet
The company below, then.

The reaction of the listener is to leap to his feet and head for the stairs – notice the abrupt transition to the listener and the placing of the *"then"* at the end of the sentence, as if the Duke has, for once, and only momentarily, lost the initiative. The Duke continues talking, seemingly unaware of the reaction his revelation has had on his audience.

*   I repeat,*
The Count your master's known munificence
Is ample warrant that no just pretense
Of mine for dowry will be disallowed;
Though his fair daughter's self, as I avowed
At starting, is my object.

The Duke reverts to an earlier topic of conversation, as if the revelation just made can go unremarked. The reason for the listener's visit is made clear – he has come to broker a new marriage between his master, the Count, and the Duke. The *"last Duchess"* is, indeed, the latest in a chain. The Duke is asserting that he is sure his demand for a dowry for the girl (the bridal gift from a father to the future son-in-law) will be sufficiently generous although, he insists, the girl herself is what he wants – but the word *"object"* belies this. Browning is punning on "*object*" as in "*objective*" or goal, and "*object*" as "*thing*". She is just a trophy to him.

> *Nay, we'll go*
> *Together down, sir. Notice Neptune, though,*
> *Taming a sea-horse, thought a rarity,*
> *Which Claus of Innsbruck cast in bronze for me!*

The envoy appears to make a further move to get away but is stayed by the Duke, shown by the *syntax* that places "*Together*" at the beginning of the line, – "*Nay, we'll go/Together down.*" As they leave, the Duke points out another "*object*" (or "*objet d'art*" as Browning is punning) – a statue of Neptune, God of the Sea, taming a seahorse. This image is deliberately ambiguous. As God of the Sea, Neptune rode huge horses with the tails of fish, as depicted in classical art, as at:
https://en.wikipedia.org/wiki/Neptune_(mythology)#/media/File:Sousse_neptune.jpg

But to us, a seahorse is a tiny fish, conjuring up the image of a powerful man dominating a much weaker creature – just as the Duke has dominated, and ultimately killed, his Duchess. To the Duke, she was a possession to reflect his power and status, as much as the painting by a famous artist or a bronze by a famous sculptor.

"*Home-Thoughts, from Abroad*" – Robert Browning

This is Browning's most famous lyric poem. In classical times, a lyric poem was originally a poem set to music played on a *lyre*, a form of small harp, but came to be applied to any (short) poem which has as its theme love, or explores and expresses the thoughts and feelings of the poet. It is essentially *non-narrative*; there is no story being told. The poem shows Browning's debt to the Romantics – the poetic movement that immediately preceded the Victorians, of whom the main exponents were Wordsworth, Byron, Coleridge, Shelley and Keats. The central theme of their poetry is the transcendent power of Nature and the value and authenticity of human emotions and feelings in the face of an increasingly rational and scientific approach to the world. They are spiritual, but not religious. The detailed references to the observed world and the emotional response to nature are hallmarks of the Romantic approach.

Browning's poem was published in 1845 in "*Dramatic Romances and Lyrics*", number VII in a series of pamphlets containing plays and poems under the collective title "*Bells and Pomegranates*" – a reference to the Bible in which Aaron (Moses's brother) is described as having a robe hemmed with ornaments of this shape. Browning explained his choice of this reference as: "*the hem of the robe of the high priest*" to indicate "*the mixture of music with discoursing, sound with sense, poetry with thought.*"

Browning travelled to Italy for the first time in the late 1830s and again in the early 1840s. In spite of the message of the poem, Browning was very fond of Italy and he and Elizabeth made their home there after their marriage, although they returned to England for family visits. The poem evokes the sights and sounds of the English countryside and is infused with nostalgia. Note how the irregular metric pattern is used to match the poet's emotions. Note also the characteristic use of *enjambment* and *caesura*.

Oh, to be in England
Now that April's there,
And whoever wakes in England
Sees, some morning, unaware,
That the lowest boughs and the brushwood sheaf
Round the elm-tree bole are in tiny leaf,
While the chaffinch sings on the orchard bough
In England—now!

The poem opens with an exclamation, as if the emotion of longing has spilled out of him spontaneously. The word *"there"* is odd – in fact, it is often misquoted as *"here"*. After all, it is April in Italy as well. So, a contrast is made immediately – April in Italy is of quite a different quality, almost not like April at all. He is, of course, comparing the more temperate climate of England with the Mediterranean climate of Italy, to the latter's disadvantage. In England, spring comes stealthily (*"unaware"*), the leaves appearing as if overnight on the elm-trees and the surrounding bushes and the chaffinch (a small, pink-breasted songbird) has begun singing.

The *octet* is in *trimetre* for the first three lines, but as the emotion grows and he warms to his subject, the lines lengthen to *tetrametre*. He ends it with another exclamation, using a *dimetre*, as if his emotions have overwhelmed him and he cannot go on. The rhyme scheme is regular – *ababccdd* – which again matches the growing excitement as the rhymes become more closely packed.

However, one thought leads to another, as May follows April, the subject of the next *octet*:

And after April, when May follows,
And the whitethroat builds, and all the swallows!

The references here are to two birds – the whitethroat and swallow - which migrate to England in the spring to breed – another symbol of how England's seasons change. The two lines form an incomplete sentence, as if his memories are tumbling from him uncontrolled.

Hark, where my blossomed pear-tree in the hedge
Leans to the field and scatters on the clover
Blossoms and dewdrops—at the bent spray's edge—
That's the wise thrush; he sings each song twice over,
Lest you should think he never could recapture
The first fine careless rapture!

The poet asks us to *"Listen!"* to the sound of a thrush in his garden (*"**my** blossomed…"*). The scene is described in detail, as if recalling an actual event: the thrush is sitting at the end of a spray of the pear-tree, which is growing in a hedge (perhaps the boundary of his garden) and leaning over into the neighbouring field, where it drops its *"Blossoms and dewdrops"* onto the clover crop below. Browning uses the subordination of this long sentence, between *"Hark!"* and *"That's the wise thrush;"* to lead us through the image of the blossoming pear-tree in the hedge, up and out over the field to where the thrush perches on the out-flung branch. Browning's observation is accurate – the song thrush (*turdus philomelus*) prefers to sing perched at the end of a branch. Its song is characterised by the repetition of notes and phrases. The thrush is *"wise"* because it repeats itself to make sure it doesn't forget its song - and so that we do not presume that it cannot reproduce the first, glorious outpouring of its song.

The lines are now in the longer *iambic pentametre* as his vision of England expands. The rhyme scheme subtly alters, but remains regular, the rhyming couplets now used for emphasis: *aabcbcdd*.

And though the fields look rough with hoary dew,
All will be gay when noontide wakes anew
The buttercups, the little children's dower
—Far brighter than this gaudy melon-flower!

The recollections continue in the final quatrain, with its *rhyming couplets*, with the image of a late *"hoar"* frost; possibly the whiteness of the dew is being likened to hoar-frost, covering the fields. However, by midday it will have warmed up and burnt off the dew, or frost, and the buttercups will open. The bright yellow buttercups are described as a gift or *dowry* to children – from the sun, possibly, as they reflect its yellow light. A favourite game of children used to be to test if you "liked butter" by holding a buttercup under the chin to see if it reflected yellow. It usually does, as the inside of a buttercup petal is shiny and light reflective. The buttercup is compared with the exotic *"melon flower"*, which is also yellow and much larger than a buttercup. The melon is a member of the same botanical family as cucumbers and squash but they do not grow naturally in England as it is too cold.

There is some xenophobia here perhaps. The Colonial British (although Italy was never a colony) prided themselves on their restraint and order; they saw themselves as "civilising" the peoples they came into contact with. Browning dismisses the *"gaudy"* melon flower for being too exotic, too extravagant and showy, preferring the unassuming native wildflower of England.

However, Browning was well-travelled and cosmopolitan, and, at this time, had little reason to love the "British Public"; the reaction to his poetry, and in particular the long poem *"Sordello"* published in 1840, was generally negative and was criticised for its obscurity. This criticism effectively hampered his career for years - after 1844 he published very little until late in life, and many of the poems now recognised as being his greatest (apart from the epic *"The Ring and the Book"* (1869)) pre-date his marriage and emigration to Italy.

Lines from this poem have been referenced by many poets, showing its enduring, and endearing, influence over time. It ranked number 42 in the Nation's 100 Favourite Poems poll carried out by the BBC (*"My Last Duchess"* was at 69); there is a song by the same name by Clifford T Ward published in the 1970s; a poem by the novelist John Buchan; Carol Anne Duffy, the poet Laureate, named her autobiographical collection of love poems *"Rapture"* and quotes the poem in her dedication; Thomas Hardy's *"The Darkling Thrush"* references it; Rupert Brooke, poet of the First World War, echoes its sentiments in *"The Soldier"*.

"Meeting at Night" – Robert Browning

Another of Browning's lyrical poems, published in *Dramatic Romances and Lyrics* (1845) and written during his courtship of EBB. The poem imagines a lover travelling towards a secret meeting with his beloved, and, given the clandestine nature of Browning's and EBB's relationship, the poem is autobiographical in its evocation of the emotions of the lovers, if not the geography of their meetings – which took place in London and not in a farmhouse near the sea.

The sea is often a metaphor for transformation or new beginnings. This journey may reflect the significant upset to both their lives as a result of their meeting, as well as the promise of a new life together. Also, Browning spent some years before they met travelling in Europe, and so would have returned home to England by boat. The description of the landscape suggests pleasure in being "home" as well as eagerness to be reunited with the beloved, echoing the sentiments of *"Home-Thoughts…"*

The poem is written in loose *iambic tetrametre,* often used for lyrics as it retains the sing-song rhythm and line-length of earlier songs, as well as propelling the movement forward. Browning varies the metric feet, as in his other poems, to create particular effects – emphasising certain words. The rhyme scheme – *abccba* –is *chiastic*. It reverses at the midpoint of the sestet and each stanza is enclosed (sometimes called *"envelope structure"*) by the first and last rhyme.

I
*The **grey sea** and the **long** black **land**;*
*And the **yell**ow **half**-moon **large** and **low**;*
*And the **startled** little **waves** that **leap***
*In **fiery ring**lets **from** their **sleep**,*

"Love in a Life" – Robert Browning

The poem was published in the volume *"Men and Women"* in 1855, which also contained the similarly named *"Life in Love"*. This also has separation as its theme. The volume was dedicated to Elizabeth and the poems were the first published works of Browning for five years.

Written during the couples' time in Italy, the setting is touchingly domestic, with references to their furniture and EBB's dress. The conceit[17] is that the poet (Browning) is searching through their house, looking for his beloved (EBB) – but she seems to elude him.

The poem is written in two stanzas with matching metric patterns – a *tercet* (three lines) in *dimetre* (two strong beats), followed by a *tercet* in *tetrameter* (four strong beats), ending with a couplet in *pentametre* (five strong beats)– a highly unusual pattern. In stanza one, it reflects the stages of his search: the short lines as he moves from place to place, hurriedly searching; the longer lines as his gaze sweeps the room and he realises that she has been there but is now gone; finally, a reflection on the meaning of her presence on him and his life – that she enriches it immeasurably.

I
Room after room,
I hunt the house through
We inhabit together.
Heart, fear nothing, for, heart, thou shalt find her
Next time, herself! not the trouble behind her
Left in the curtain, the couch's perfume!
As she brushed it, the cornice-wreath blossomed anew:
Yon looking-glass gleamed at the wave of her feather.

---

[17] *Conceit* – a type of metaphor, often fanciful or elaborate

The opening places us in the room with Browning as he looks for Elizabeth. The *syntax* is awkward, but, as is common with Browning, it is ordered so as to present events to us in a particular hierarchy – we focus on the room, then him hunting, then the where, which gives the search significance. He is not concerned – his *"heart"* is sure that he will find her. *"Heart"* is *synecdoche* – using a part (of himself) as the whole and a familiar poetic usage to indicate the location of the emotion of love. He believes she has just left the room, leaving signs of her presence behind. *"Trouble"* is used here in the sense of *"disturbance"* as in *"troubled waters"*. He can smell her perfume in the curtains and the couch. He then *eulogises* (praises) Elizabeth as if she were some goddess who can animate objects – the flowery decoration of the *"cornice"* (a border where the walls of a room meet the ceiling) blossom as her dress touches it, and a mirror *gleams* with the reflection of a *feather* in her hair (feathers in the hair were a popular Victorian adornment).

II

Yet the day wears,
And door succeeds door;
I try the fresh fortune

The poet is conscious that it is getting late and he still hasn't found her. The short lines of the opening *tercet* reflect his growing urgency and concern as he continues his hunt, as does the repeated *"door after door"*.

Range the wide house from the wing to the centre.
Still the same chance! she goes out as I enter.
Spend my whole day in the quest, who cares?

The lines of the following *tercet* lengthen as he extends his search. He decides to be methodical and search from the outer reaches of the house into the centre. But she still eludes him, seeming to be just leaving the room as he enters. His

A free bird on that lilac bush
Outside the lattice heard
He listened long — there came a hush
He dropped an answering word —

The prisoner to the free replied

The moment of anticipation of an answering call is conveyed by the use of the hyphen after "*long –* "and again after "*word – "*. Notice also the alliterated use of "*l*" to suggest trilling: "*tri**l**led*", "***l**ilac*", "***l**attice*", "***l**istened **l**ong*".

"I now had only to retrace" – Charlotte Bronte

The date of publication *(1934)* suggests that this is, again, a poem that has been dredged from the numerous unpublished manuscripts of the Brontes' which have been collected by various institutions and scholars. The Brontes are "big business" in the academic world – because much of their work was unpublished and the manuscripts either destroyed or scattered. Victor Neufeldt, in his *"The Poems of Charlotte Bronte: A New Text and Commentary"* (Routledge. 2015) puts the date as *"late 1846 - early 1847"*, in the same period as the fragment *"The house was still"* and the publication of *"Jane Eyre"*. This makes it too early to be a poem mourning the death of her three surviving siblings, all of whom died 1848 – 1849. There is no doubt, however, that the poem is about loss, and at the end, there is a strong suggestion that it is about death. Another possibility, which the idea of *"retracing"* supports, is that this is a reference to her doomed infatuation with Monsieur Heger, the married owner of the school where she and Emily went to study French in 1842 - 1843 and to where she returned in 1844.

The poem suggests hopelessness, and abandonment. It combines suggestions of the loss of life and the loss of love, but in its emphasis on West and East, and the biblical references, it also has a quasi-religious overtone. It could possibly be considered as a spiritual response to the loss of faith.

The poem is again in *common* metre. It clearly evokes the changeable, stormy weather of the Yorkshire Moors which forms a backdrop to so much of the Brontes' prose and poetry.

I now had only to retrace
The long and lonely road
So lately in the rainbow chase
With fearless ardour trod

The path she is going to take will not be one taken in her imaginary worlds, populated with knights and ladies, kings and queens who live lives of noble endeavour. She is going back to her "roots."

I'll walk where my own nature would be leading:
It vexes me to choose another guide:
Where the grey flocks in ferny glens are feeding;
Where the wild wind blows on the mountain side.

The poet evokes the countryside that has sustained her all her life; she has no need for a guide to understand it. The *alliteration* emphasises her passion for the simple, natural world and her feeling that she is at one with the sheep on the hills and the wind blowing across it.

What have those lonely mountains worth revealing?
More glory and more grief than I can tell:
The earth that wakes one human heart to feeling
Can centre both the worlds of Heaven and Hell.

The rhetorical question anticipates the cynicism of the "real world" of *"wealth and learning"* about the value of nature to teach. Her robust response (in the emphatic repetition of *"more"*) is that it can teach us everything about triumph and failure – *"glory and ...grief"*. If your heart is receptive, the power of nature can make sense of the whole world and everything within it.

"Remember" – Christina Rossetti

Critics of Christina Rossetti refer to her "ambiguity", her teasing, questioning voice which challenges the readers' interpretation of her poems and the apparent conflicts in her approach to themes of, in particular, spirituality and sexuality. The long poem, "*Goblin Market*", published in 1862, best exemplifies these features of her poetry, but they are evident, too, in her shorter works. Rossetti's perspective is often from one dead, or contemplating her death. Much is infused with a sense of the loss of love, or the opportunity for love, although whether this is love in a religious or secular context is not always clear. Love and death seem at times inextricably linked. She never married, although she received proposals three times. Like EBB, she too suffered from life-long fragile health, dying from Grave's Disease, a disorder of the thyroid gland, in 1894, aged 64.

"*Remember*" is one of her most famous poems and a popular choice for reading at funerals. It is a *Petrarchan sonnet*; it is written in *iambic pentametre* and the rhyme scheme of the *octet*[18] is *abbaabba* and the *sestet*[19] *cddece*. This cyclical rhyme scheme is particularly suited to the theme of going away in death and returning in memory, as is the repetition.

Remember me when I am gone away,
Gone far away into the silent land;
When you can no more hold me by the hand,
Nor I half turn to go yet turning stay.

The poem is an address from the poet, contemplating her own death, to her lover. The reader's perspective is that of the lover's. The poem opens with an imperative, demanding that the lover

---

[18] The first **eight** lines
[19] The final **six** lines

"*Remember*" her. The references to "*the silent land*" and "*hold... by the hand*" echoes Orpheus's descent into the Underworld, to reclaim his dead Eurydice. The finality of death, as opposed to a parting in life, is expressed with the phrase "*half-turn to go yet turning stay*". In life, you can change your mind about leaving; in death, it is a one-way street.

Remember me when no more day by day
You tell me of our future that you plann'd:
Only remember me; you understand
It will be late to counsel then or pray.

Death negates future plans. She speaks as if she has been aware of this always; it is "*our future*" but only he ("*you*") seems to have planned it. It was not a joint activity, suggesting its futility. All the lover can do is "*remember*" – it will be too late to give her advice or have hope for the future.

The *volta* at the *sestet* indicates a new realisation by the poet and a shift in the advice to the lover, indicated by the word "*Yet*":

Yet if you should forget me for a while
And afterwards remember, do not grieve:
For if the darkness and corruption leave
A vestige of the thoughts that once I had,
Better by far you should forget and smile
Than that you should remember and be sad.

She admits the possibility that her lover will, at times, forget her, but that he should not feel badly about it. Although her physical self is now in the darkness of the grave and decomposing ("*corruption*"), she hopes that something of her mind and spirit will remain to sustain him and that when he *does* remember her, he is happy to do so.

Although there is something self-indulgent about imagining yourself looking down on the people left behind after you have gone (and apparently imagining your own funeral, surrounded by your mourning friends and family, is common), ultimately the message is one of selflessness, in that she wishes him to be happy in his remembrance.

"Echo" – Christina Rossetti

The title of the poem gives a clue as to the ideas in the poem. Echo was a nymph who lived on Mt Cithaeron, where Zeus was in the habit of consorting with other nymphs, being a serial womaniser. His wife, Hera, became jealous and arrived to catch him in the act. However, Echo distracted her by constantly talking. When Juno realised the nymph's treachery, she condemned her to being unable to speak, except for the last few words of those spoken to her. The "echo" in the poem is from a dead soul to one still living whom the poet craves would "*Come back*". The poem conveys an anguished sense of loss, and Rossetti may also be drawing on the story of Echo after she is cursed by Hera. Echo falls in love with a beautiful mortal, Narcissus, but is unable to tell him of her love. She can only echo the ends of his words. He rejects her, falling in love with his own reflection in a stream and being turned into the white flower of the same name. The poet uses water imagery throughout. Echoes, in reality, call back the words spoken by the listener and there is a strong identification of the lost love with the poet, as if they were two souls in one body – *"My very life again"*.

There is another strong influence at work in this poem. Rossetti was familiar with the works of Dante Alighieri, an Italian poet of the late 13th century. In his masterpiece, "*La Divina Commedia*", the poet travels to the Underworld, led by the Roman poet, Virgil. Whilst there, he meets his beloved, Beatrice, who leads him to the gates of Paradise. Beatrice was a real woman whom Dante first knew as a child, but only met on an very few occasions, both he and she marrying others. She died at the age of 24 – the age at which Rossetti wrote this poem.

Rossetti was innovative in her use of varied metre to expand the emotional range of her verse, a feature which was met with some puzzlement by her contemporary critics, used to the regular rhythm and rhyme of mainstream Victorian verse.

The poem is written in *iambic pentametre*, with the 4th and 5th lines between them creating a full line. The initial *iamb* is inverted to form a *trochee* (**Tum**-ti rather than Ti-**Tum**) which, together with the *anaphora* on *"Come"*, gives the poem its pleading tone.

> *Come to me in the silence of the night;*
> > *Come in the speaking silence of a dream;*
>
> *Come with soft rounded cheeks and eyes as bright*
> > *As sunlight on a stream;*
>
> *Come back in tears,*
> *O memory, hope, love of finished years.*

The poet pleads for the lover to return from the dead and speak to (her) in (her) dreams. The gender of both speaker and lover is indeterminate – *"rounded cheeks"* is perhaps more suggestive of a woman or a very young man. The poet uses an *oxymoron*[20] to express the paradox of dreams – *"speaking silence"*. Dreams are silent and yet the dreamer can clearly hear voices – again like an echo, which is not real in itself. The image of *"sunlight on a stream"* suggests the sparkle of sunlight on water, emphasised by the *alliteration*. This vibrant image shifts as the glitter turns to that of *"tears"*. Whether they are the tears of the poet or the lover's is deliberately ambiguous, showing mutual sorrow at parting. The longed-for visitor brings with it *"memory, hope, love"* which were promises when alive, but are now *"finished"*. The rhyme scheme (*ababcc*) also plays on opposing themes: *"night/bright"*, *"dream/stream"*.

---

[20] Two words juxtaposed which appear to contradict one another, as in *"bitter sweet"* or *"cold fire"*. Shakespeare littered *"Romeo and Juliet"* with oxymorons, underpinning the theme of two opposites uniting.

Oh dream how sweet, too sweet, too bitter sweet,
    Whose wakening should have been in Paradise,
Where souls brimfull of love abide and meet;
    Where thirsting longing eyes
    Watch the slow door
That opening, letting in, lets out no more.

The poet wakes up as the dream fades. The sense of desolation, being cheated by the dream, is expressed by the repeated *"sweet"* as it moves from *"how sweet"* (it is real) to *"too sweet* (it cannot be real) to the oxymoron *"bitter sweet"* (it is not real, and painful, but better than nothing). The reuniting of the loved ones should have ended in heaven, with her dying. In *Paradise* is where those parted by death meet and live together again. The water imagery continues with *"brimfull"*, meaning a vessel full of water about to overflow, in contrast to the desolate place where they are apart and are parched, *"thirsting"* for one another. The parted souls wait by the Gates of Paradise for them to open and allow their loved ones through into heaven, from which they never return. There is no need for "echoes".

Yet come to me in dreams, that I may live
    My very life again tho' cold in death:
Come back to me in dreams, that I may give
    Pulse for pulse, breath for breath:
    Speak low, lean low,
As long ago, my love, how long ago.

In spite of the pain of parting on awakening, the poet still longs for the loved one to come to (her) in (her) dreams, as only then is she able to relive the life that they enjoyed together, even though it is but a cold *"echo"* of that life. In her dreams, the beloved and (she) can be together as one again, as they used to be in life.

The ideas of a *liminal space* are similar to those in "*Remember me*", with the fusion of life and death, as if there is only a thin veil between the two and that in dreams and memory you can pass between them, recapturing not just the emotional intensity of the relationship but the physical intimacy as well.

"May" – Christina Rossetti

This poem is deceptively simple. It is a highy contrived, truncated *sonnet* of thirteen lines long. Other than the loss of the last line, it conforms to the sonnet form closely, with a *volta* at the ninth line and a regular, tight, rhyme scheme (*aabbccdd aabbb*). The loss of the last line to complete the form is a reflection of its theme, which is unfulfillment, or the fading of a promise for the future.

There is a mystery at the heart of the poem, but also an ambiguity. The poet *"cannot tell"* the reader what has happened – *"came to pass"*. It is not immediately clear whether this means *"cannot"* as in *"I am not allowed to"*, or *"cannot"* as in *"I do not know"*. The oppostion created by the phrase *"But this I know..."* (as in *"I don't know **that**, but I **do** know this..."*), together with the slight variation in this repeated phrase at the *volta,* suggests the latter, which subtly changes the meaning of the whole. It becomes not a knowing secret, that is being kept from the reader, but an expression of ignorance and bewilderment at what has happened.

I cannot tell you how it was;
But this I know: it came to pass
Upon a bright and breezy day
When May was young; ah, pleasant May!
As yet the poppies were not born
Between the blades of tender corn;
The last eggs had not hatched as yet,
Nor any bird forgone its mate.

The imagery is of promise and fulfilment. The weather is sunny, but does not have the warmth of summer – it is still early May. The exclamation *"ah...!"* expresses the poet's pleasure at the promise May brings. The corn in the fields has only just started to grow and the field poppies, which will bloom in autumn, cannot even be seen as yet. The birds are still nesting, with eggs still in the nest, and the pairs of birds have not yet parted, which they do after nesting in summer. The imagery is suggestive of incipient growth and promise of things to come – the warmth of summer, the fruitfulness of autumn, new life in the fledged birds, domestic happiness. This suggests that the *"it"* of the first line is a feeling of hope for the future, maybe of love blossoming. At the *volta*, this optimistic outlook changes.

I cannot tell you what it was;
But this I know: it did but pass.
It passed away with sunny May,
With all sweet things it passed away,
And left me old, and cold, and grey.

The opening phrase is repeated, with the variation from *"how"* to *"what"* – the poet still does not know *"what"* it was that she felt on that sunny day, *"But"* she does *"know"* that whatever it was, it went away (*"passed"*) like a cloud passing in front of the sun. With it, it took all the sweet promise of the May day with it, leaving the day sunless and dark and her lifeless. The contrast between the fruitful imagery of the *octet* and the increasing desolation of the *sestet* is conveyed by the subtle shift in meaning of the word *"pass"*, from *"happened"* to *"go"* as in *"passed away"*; the intoning of *"pass/passed/passed"*; the rhyme of *"was"* and *"pass"*, and the final *tercet*'s rhyme of *"May/away/grey"*, which embodies the now hopeless future. As Rossetti says, she cannot, or will not, tell what it is that brought her such feelings of hope and promise for the future. Maybe it was love. All that she knows is that the feeling was fleeting, and that with its passing, she is left diminished.

"A Birthday" – Christina Rossetti

Another famous poem by Rossetti, often anthologised, particularly in children's collections of poetry, on account of its song-like repetition and rhythm and its vivid imagery. This poem sustains its buoyant, joyous tone throughout and seems a world away from the poetry of loss and longing that characterises the others in the selection. This seems to be the poetry of fulfilled and reciprocated love. The title is, to an extent, a misleading pun. The poem is not about *"A Birthday"*, but about a "Birth Day" – the day on which the poet is "born" into an enhanced reality because her lover comes to her.

The poem is deceptively simple. In fact, the imagery is rich and layered, with multiple references. The imagery in the first stanza is drawn from nature; in the second, the imagery reflects royal pageantry and harks back to the Medievalism which was a feature of the Pre-Raphaelite painters, of whom Dante Gabriel Rossetti, Christina's brother, was a member. The imagery is also reminiscent of the Song of Solomon, a poem found in the Hebrew bible and the Old Testament, as is the use of repetition. The Song is, primarily, an erotic love song between two lovers using imagery drawn from the landscape of, notably, Lebanon, as well as the contents of royal palaces. However, it is interpreted by Hebrew scholars as a metaphor for the love of God for Israel and by Christians as Christ's (the Bridegroom's) love for the Christian church (the Bride). This fusion of the sacred and the profane (secular) is a feature of much of Rossetti's poetry. She was brought up as a Catholic by her Italian parents and much of her poetry is overtly religious in theme. An article on her religious poetry, which comments on *"A Birthday"*, can be found at www.bl.uk/romantics-and-victorians/articles/christina-rossetti-religious-poetry. Rossetti's poem also contains classical illusions.

The poem is made up of two *octets* in regular *iambic tetrametere*, which give it a lilting, lyrical quality, reflective of her feeling of ecstasy. The rhyme scheme is also regular – *abcb dcec* – which gives it a tight, controlled construction, evocative of the feeling of assurance and confidence contained in the final lines of each stanza.

> *My heart is like a singing bird*
> > *Whose nest is in a water'd shoot;*
>
> *My heart is like an apple-tree*
> > *Whose boughs are bent with thickset fruit;*
>
> *My heart is like a rainbow shell*
> > *That paddles in a halcyon sea;*
>
> *My heart is gladder than all these*
> > *Because my love is come to me.*

The poet chooses three images from nature to explore her feelings of love, whether love for another or for Christ. *"Water"* is an image of life; the bird sings because it is bringing forth new life from its nest, which in turn is given life by the water. This idea of new growth gives way to the idea of fulfilment in the apples of autumn, so plentiful that they weigh down the boughs of the apple trees. The final image is of peace, as she compares her feelings to the rainbow-hued shell of a creature that lives in the sea – possibly an abalone shell, which is multi-coloured. The word *"paddles"* is childlike and innocent, as if the creature is safe and secure as it moves around its watery habitat. Rainbows are a symbol of peace – God's promise after the Flood that he would never punish Man again in such a way – and *"halcyon"* is the classical name for the Kingfisher, a bright blue and orange river bird. *"Halcyon"* was the name given by the Greeks to the bird, which was believed to create a floating nest on the sea in which to lay its eggs. This signalled calm weather – as in *"halcyon days"* for a period of calm. The poet's heart is "gladder" than any of these contented images, however, because of the arrival of her beloved.

> Raise me a dais of silk and down;
> > Hang it with vair and purple dyes;
> Carve it in doves and pomegranates,
> > And peacocks with a hundred eyes;
> Work it in gold and silver grapes,
> > In leaves and silver fleurs-de-lys;
> Because the birthday of my life
> > Is come, my love is come to me.

On the arrival of the beloved, the imagery becomes rich and opulent, suggesting excess. The simple repetition of *"My heart"* gives way to imperatives – *"Raise"*, *"Carve"*, *"Work"* – as she demands that people celebrate and bear tribute to the two of them, as if to royalty, in surroundings befitting this momentous occasion – the start of her real life. The idea of this new life being also a marriage is contained in the word *"dais"* on which she wishes to be raised. It was the custom to place the bride and groom on a raised platform in front of their guests, a custom which remains today when the bridal party sits at the "top table".

The *"dais"* is to be covered with the most expensive fabrics; purple was a colour reserved for royalty and *"vair"* was a fur cloak made up of the skins of, probably, squirrels, sewn together to show an alternating pattern of the front and back of the animal, so as to give a variegated pattern. It is a word from Heraldry, again suggesting the medieval. This *"dais"* is made of wood and she demands that it be decorated with designs of *"doves"* – symbols of peace, as this was the bird that brought back the olive branch to Noah after the Flood – and *"pomegranates"* – symbols of fertility, as it contains hundreds of seeds. Both are mentioned repeatedly to describe the lovers in the Song of Solomon, as in *"thou has dove's eyes"* and *"thy temples* (forehead) *are like pomegranates"*. *"Peacocks"* are traditionally royal birds; they are associated with the Queen of the Gods, Hera, and were served to royalty during the medieval period at banquets. They have also been adopted by Christian iconography as symbols of everlasting life. In her newly exulted state, the poet wants real grapes and their vines to be replaced with decorations in gold and silver. The *"fleur-de-lys"* is a heraldic symbol of royalty, in both Italy and France, and is common in medieval tapestry and manuscripts. It is often (I believe mistakenly) translated as a *"flower of the lily"* and the etymology is still disputed. It is more probably an iris.

The opulence of the imagery suggests that she is being born anew, out of an ordinary life into one where the natural world pours its bounty upon her. She wants this altered state to be recognised with all the pomp and trappings usually associated with a royal marriage.

"Somewhere or Other" – Christina Rossetti

This poem is once again full of yearning for a soul mate. In spite of disappointment, the poet continues to hope that *"somewhere"* out there is someone, or something, that she can join with and find her love reciprocated. Whether this is a secular or spiritual joining is again left ambiguous, but the imagery is of this world and rooted in familiar sights and sounds.

Although there is an underlying *iambic tetrametre* rhythm, most clearly in the second line of each stanza, there is considerable variation to allow for free expressions of her emotions. The rhyme scheme is regular – *ababcdcdefef* – which suggest a Shakespearean sonnet. However, there is no finishing couplet, and no *volta*. Instead, the repeated opening of the second and third *quatrains* shows little development in the argument through the poem – which is indeed a theme, as the poet has so far searched in vain and is close to despair.

Somewhere or other there must surely be
The face not seen, the voice not heard,
The heart that not yet—never yet—ah me!
Made answer to my word.

The poet begins in disbelief; surely there is someone, or something, out there to be found and which will respond to her need for a soul mate? The extent of her longing is clearly expressed in the third line, where her longing breaks through, the rhythm becomes uneven and the line lengthens. The images of the hidden face, the silent voice and hearts beating together is familiar from *"Remember Me"* or *"Echo"*.

Somewhere or other, may be near or far;
Past land and sea, clean out of sight;

Beyond the wandering moon, beyond the star
That tracks her night by night.

Her continuing search is conveyed through the repetition. In this stanza she searches *"far"*; however far away it might be, the looked for one is out there. She identifies herself with the *"star"* that follows the moon, but never catches it. This is the planet Venus, named after the Goddess of Love, which often appears in close proximity to the moon.

Somewhere or other, may be far or near;
With just a wall, a hedge, between;
With just the last leaves of the dying year
Fallen on a turf grown green.

The first line of the second quatrain is repeated, but with a change of word order, as the search now comes *"near"*; maybe the one looked for is close at hand, separated from the seeker by only a garden hedge or wall. The final image seems to be one of the endless cycle of the seasons, as autumn gives way to winter and then to spring, in much the same way as her search goes on for ever. The poem also seems to end irresolutely.

"At an Inn" – Thomas Hardy

It is a significant jump from Rossetti to Hardy, as the number of skipped pages in the anthology suggests. On the way, the selection has missed significant poets such as Matthew Arnold and GM Hopkins, and does not look forward to the end of the century by covering early Yeats, Kipling or AE Housman. One can only assume that the selection is based on the need to find links between the poets for the purpose of exam questions! To give you a more comprehensive view of the complete sweep of the poetry of the Victorians, do read "*Dover Beach*" by Matthew Arnold, which contemplates a world without Faith, and "*The Windhover*" by Gerard Manley Hopkins, one of the greatest poems ever written. Leaving GMH out of this selection is, frankly, unforgivable. But he writes about Christ and God - and in this secular, yet multicultural, world perhaps they thought he was too scary to tackle! He is also hard to compare with other poets, as he is simply unique.

Hardy is probably better known for his novels than for his poetry. In fact, he did not return to writing poetry until the completion of his last novel, "*Jude the Obscure*", in 1895. His novels - particularly "*Tess of the D'Ubervilles*" and "*Jude the Obscure*" - are acknowledged as some of the best novels of the era, challenging Victorian bourgeois values, exploring the plight of women and Victorian sexual hypocrisy, and the effects of the Industrial Revolution on the rural poor. I would describe his poetry as "highly variable". There is a useful introduction to Hardy produced by AQA at http://filestore.aqa.org.uk/resources/english/AQA-7716-7717-TRAGEDY-HARDY.PDF

It is suggested that the poem "*At an Inn*" is based on the relationship between Florence Henniker and Hardy and a visit to the George Hotel in Winchester. Hardy first met Florence in 1893, when his marriage was in trouble, and he appears to have fallen in love with her. However, there is no suggestion that they had a sexual relationship; she was married to an army officer and rejected Hardy's advances. They corresponded for 30 years, until her death in 1923, and even wrote a short story together. He described her in his letters as *"One rare, fair woman"*.

The poem tells of a misunderstanding, thoughts of what might have been and lost opportunities. It is written in regular, alternating *iambic trimetre* and *iambic dimetre* lines with a regular rhyming pattern of *ababcdcd*. This gives it a conversational feel – as if he is recounting a story known to them both and that it is light-hearted and reminiscent. However, the manipulation of the accented beats on particular words reveals the deep feelings running below the surface.

When we as strangers sought
Their catering care,
Veiled smiles bespoke their thought
Of what we were.
They warmed as they opined
Us more than friends--
That we had all resigned
For love's dear ends.

There is something rather unfortunate about the phrase *"catering care"*. Is it ironic? The use of the alliteration for such a mundane phrase suggests it might be – contrasting the knowing smiles and looks of the servants with the emotional intensity he is feeling. It could, of course, just be bad. However, the contrast between the two *"strangers"* and idle gossipers is clearly present in the way the focus of the stanza switches between the two groups: *"we as strangers/Their...care"*; *"Veiled smiles/what we were"*; *"they opined/Us more than friends"*. What the servants are thinking is made explicit in the last two lines – they think that the two are lovers, not married to one another, who have come to the hotel for an assignation. This would have been quite scandalous even in late Victorian England.

And that swift sympathy
With living love
Which quicks the world--maybe
The spheres above,
Made them our ministers,
Moved them to say,
"Ah, God, that bliss like theirs
Would flush our day!"

If there is an initial resentment or annoyance at the prurience of the servants, then Hardy becomes more charitable towards them in the next stanza. He recognises in them a response ("*swift sympathy*") to the possibility that the two visitors are lovers and transforms them into guardian angels ("*ministers*") who bless their supposed love and hope for similar fortune. "*Ministers*" is also a pun – servants "(ad)*minister*" to their guests. So maybe his approach is wryly humorous or sarcastic?

And we were left alone
As Love's own pair;
Yet never the love-light shone
Between us there!
But that which chilled the breath
Of afternoon,
And palsied unto death
The pane-fly's tune.

In the third stanza, the true relationship between the two is revealed. They've been left alone by the servants, to give the "Lovers" some privacy, but Hardy tells us quite forcibly, with the use of the exclamation mark, that they were not Lovers – far from it. There is a coldness between them that affects the very air they breathe, even killing a poor fly buzzing at the window. Frosty indeed. *"love-light"*, meaning the light of love in someone's eyes, was a relatively new word at this time – the first recorded use of it is in 1823.

The kiss their zeal foretold,
And now deemed come,
Came not: within his hold
Love lingered numb.
Why cast he on our port
A bloom not ours?
Why shaped us for his sport
In after-hours?

The servants have been mistaken about the relationship between the two – there is no kissing. *"Love"*, now personified, fails to deliver on the promise – he is *"numb"*, staying at home. The rhetorical questions from Hardy show his frustration – they have opportunity, but the feeling is missing. Love has made them look the part, but as if toying with them (*"sport"*), he does not deliver. *"Port"* here means the place where they are staying – another odd word to sustain the rhyme – as is *"after hours"*, perhaps.

As we seemed we were not
That day afar,
And now we seem not what
We aching are.
O severing sea and land,
O laws of men,
Ere death, once let us stand
As we stood then!

The final stanza shifts our perspective away from the apparent present or recent past, of the visit to the Inn, as we learn that he is looking back on an incident that happened some years before – *"that day afar"*. Love has played a cruel trick on them. When they were together at the Inn, they were not what they seemed – now, they appear not to be in love, but in fact, are. But they are separated by distance and by *"laws of men"* – a reference to them both being married. Hardy's final plea is that, before they die, they stand together once more, as they did at the Inn, but this time in Love in both appearance and reality.

"I Look into my Glass" – Thomas Hardy

This poem was probably written in 1897 and published in 1898 when Hardy was 57 years old. He laments his physical deterioration as he ages. He contrasts his aging, weak body with his still-youthful feelings, which remain powerful. It is perhaps tempting to believe that this, too, is a poem about his feelings for Florence Henniker, some twenty years his junior. It was another published in *"Wessex Poems"* in 1898 – five years after his meeting with her in Dublin.

The idea of youthful feelings being frustrated by being contained within an aging *"frame"* was explored by Tennyson in one of his most beautiful, and heart-breaking, poems, *"Tithonus"* (1859), which has its origins in classical mythology. In the mythology, Eos, the goddess of dawn, steals Tithonus (and his brother, Ganymede) from Troy to be her consorts. Ganymede is later stolen from her by Zeus, to be his cup-bearer, and as a consolation, Eos asks Zeus to make the beautiful Tithonus immortal. Unfortunately, he gives him eternal life – but not eternal youth. Tithonus wastes away, growing physically older and older, while watching Eos remain young and beautiful. In the poem, Tennyson adds to the poignancy by making the "gift" come from Eos rather than Zeus.

The poem is written in a regular metric pattern of four line stanzas, the first two and the last lines being in *iambic trimetre* and the third in *iambic tetrametre*. The first two *trimetres*, with the short phrases, give it the tone, initially, of a casual observation, as if he is just thinking out loud as ideas occur to him; the third, longer, line develops the idea with increased emotion; the fourth sums up the theme of the stanza. Hardy uses the present tense, as if these thoughts have only occurred, or matter, to him now, which supports the idea that they have been prompted by a recent encounter with a younger woman.

I look into my glass,
And view my wasting skin,
And say, "Would God it came to pass
My heart had shrunk as thin!"

The poet looks at his reflection in the mirror and laments what age has done to his skin – one can imagine he is looking at wrinkles, a sagging jaw-line and the loss of youthful tone. He focuses on himself with the repeated *"my"*. He wishes, in an outburst of emotion conveyed in the extended metric line, that his heart – his capacity to feel love – had similarly begun to waste away. He gives the reason in the next stanza.

For then, I, undistrest
By hearts grown cold to me,
Could lonely wait my endless rest
With equanimity.

If his heart was unable to feel strongly any more, then he would not be bothered by people who no longer, or never did, love him (*"grown cold"*). He could wait for death, lonely, but at least at peace (*"with equanimity"*).

But Time, to make me grieve,
Part steals, lets part abide;
And shakes this fragile frame at eve
With throbbings of noontide.

Unfortunately, Time, (personified) chooses to make him miserable by removing only one half of the whole of him as he ages. The two sides are shown in the *antithesis* of the second line (*"part steals/part abide"*). Late in his life (*"at eve"*) his body is disturbed by the same kind of feelings (*"throbbings"*) he had as a young man in his prime (*"noontide"*). Peace in old age is denied him.

The conundrum remains unresolved, as in "*At the Inn*" and others of Hardy's poems. He is caught between two possibilities or states which remain unresolved. He shows an acute awareness of the human condition, but little sense that he (or we) have any answers. His appeal to "*God*" is merely a turn of phrase - Hardy was not great believer in God's providence.

"Drummer Hodge" – Thomas Hardy

The poem is set at the time of the Second Boer War (1899- 1902), the culmination of a long-running conflict between Britain, supported by forces from its Empire, and the Boers – descendants of the original Dutch settlers of southern Africa. British settlement had been advancing for some years into Boer-controlled areas, primarily to develop, initially, diamond mining, and then gold. The incoming settlers or *uitlanders*, who were by now in a majority, demanded voting rights and representation, threatening the supremacy of the original Boers. A failure to negotiate led to the declaration of war in October, 1899.

The Boer War is notorious for introducing two, tactical policies to modern warfare: *scorched earth*, whereby farms and fields were burned to prevent local support for the Boers, and the rounding up and internment of civilians, both black and white, in *concentration camps*. The latter caused thousands of deaths from starvation and disease. The war was originally supported by the British public, but as it dragged on, there was criticism, both popularly and in Parliament, of the tactics used by the Army, under Lord Kitchener, and the effect on the civilian population. The outcome of the war was the annexation of the disputed territories into the United Republic of South Africa in 1910, under British rule.

Hardy wrote a number of poems about war, as well as a novel, *"The Trumpet Major"* which had as its background the threatened invasion of England by the French during the Napoleonic Wars, a war which Hardy returned to in his epic poem *"The Dynasts"*. As a child, he was surrounded by people who could remember those wars, and he lived long enough to see the start of the Great War in 1914, a century later, prompting him to write: '*the world, having like a spider climbed to a certain height, seems slipping back to what it was long ago'*. His attitude was of general dismay at the loss of life, the incompetence of the Generals and the general futility. There is an excellent website which puts Hardy's poetry in the context of the War at www.st-andrews.ac.uk/~pvm/HardyBWar/

Hardy was much admired by the poets of the Great War, particularly Sassoon, who recognised that he shared similar attitudes to War as they did. There is a clear reference to *"Drummer Hodge"*, although the perspective and sentiment is very different, in one of the most famous poems of the early stages of the Great War, Rupert Brooke's sonnet *"The Soldier"*, which contains the lines:

If I should die, think only this of me:
That there's some corner of a foreign field
That is forever England.

A *drummer boy* was a (usually) non-combatant member of the regiment who played a drum as it advanced into battle, to help soldiers keep time marching and to signal manoeuvres. He was not always a "boy" – i.e. younger than eighteen, when he could enlist as a soldier. Some drummer boys were adults. However, the practice of recruiting young boys into the army as drummers did not cease until after the Great War. Drummer boys were popular subjects of Victorian paintings, which were often sentimental. It is possible that in choosing the subject matter, Hardy was remembering an atrocity carried out during the Battle of Isandlwana during the Anglo-Zulu war of 1879 when the British attempted to colonise lands belonging to Zulu tribes in what is modern South Africa. On returning to camp, part of the regiment discovered that it had been overrun by the Zulus in their absence and everyone killed. The drummer boys were reportedly hung on hooks and disembowelled. Research suggests that the youngest was 16.

The vast majority of soldiers killed in combat overseas were buried near to where they fell and this continued until after the Great War and into the Second World War. Due to sheer numbers and logistics, there was no way of transporting the bodies back home before they decomposed, particularly during a war. The images of soldiers returning for burial in coffins draped in flags is a modern one, made possible by air transport.

The poem is written as a *ballad*, with regular alternating lines of *iambic tetrametre* and *iambic trimetre*, like a drumbeat, the insistent rhythm supported by the regular *ababab* rhyme scheme. Thus, the pathos of the subject matter is offset by this relentless structure, bringing a sense of irony and heightening the emotion.

They throw in Drummer Hodge, to rest
Uncoffined -- just as found:
His landmark is a kopje-crest
That breaks the veldt around:
And foreign constellations west
Each night above his mound.

The poem opens *in media res* – an action has happened before the poem starts, but the focus is on the aftermath. The callousness of the war in its denial of individual humanity and identity is initially conveyed by the opening *"They"*. Who are *"They?"* Presumably, those who were his comrades up until the moment of his death. The casual verb *"throw"*, used to describe the action of putting the body in the ground, and the lack of specifics as to where they throw him *"in"* serve to emphasise that *"Drummer Hodge"* is but one of many. Even the name, *"Hodge"*, which has been interpreted as Hardy giving the dead man the dignity of an identity, was an English equivalent of *"John Doe"* – the name given to unknown dead males.

The positioning of the word *"rest"* at the end of the line suggests an ironic pun – *"rest"* in the sense of "taking a break" and *"rest"* as in being "laid to rest". The enjambment makes the meaning clear, with its emphasis on *"Uncoffined"*, an archaic usage, perhaps suggesting that this war is like those that have gone before in its wastage of young lives. The hyphenated *"_just as found;"* adds to the sense that this death has gone all but unnoticed – he is *"found"* dead; his actual dying is unseen and he dies alone. He is quickly buried without ceremony and they move on.

There is no memorial to him except that provided by the natural landscape, of which he is becoming a part. The use of the Afrikaans words *"kopje"* (hill) and *"veldt"* (open plains) show that he is buried in unfamiliar ground, many miles from his home, whilst unfamiliar stars wheel (*"west"* means move to the west) around him.

Young Hodge the drummer never knew --
Fresh from his Wessex home --
The meaning of the broad Karoo,
The Bush, the dusty loam,
And why uprose to nightly view
Strange stars amid the gloam.

The young village boy, who left his village in Dorset for the first, and last time, to join the army, knew nothing about the country in which he has come to rest. The *"Karoo"* is a semi-desert region in South Africa; the *"Bush"* the name given by the British to wild, unfarmed country; *"loam"* means earth. All these features are a contrast with the English countryside that Hardy knew and loved. His "Wessex", in which his novels are set and where he lived, is an area roughly equated to Dorset and parts of Hampshire and Devon. It is a landscape of rolling hills, heath, farmland and woods, a stark contrast to the hot, open savannah of parts of South Africa. Hodge, an uneducated village boy, did not know that in the southern hemisphere the constellations are different. He would have seen that they were *"strange"*, but not understood why. *"Gloam"*, referring to twilight, here seems to be used as synonymous with *gloom*, meaning dark.

Yet portion of that unknown plain
Will Hodge for ever be;
His homely Northern breast and brain
Grow to some Southern tree,
And strange-eyed constellations reign
His stars eternally.

In spite of the indifference of the stars and the landscape to the body lying beneath them, he is becoming one with them as part of the natural world. His *"Northern"*, as in Northern hemisphere, body will provide the nutrients for a tree to grow. Hardy juxtaposes earth and the heavens with the boy providing his *"breast and brain"*, gifts from the earth, to the heavenly bodies that *"reign"* above him. There is also an extraordinary switch in perspective in the last two lines. Up until now, the perspective has been that of Hodge; he has been looking at the stars and wondering why they are *"strange"*, it is his body that gives life to the tree. But the compound adjective *"strange-eyed"* is from the stars' perspective – they are looking down on him as he gazes back at them. This reciprocation unites the two, bringing a kind of reconciliation and peace to his final resting place.

"A Wife in London" - Thomas Hardy

This is another poem about the Boer War. A wife receives two communications in quick succession. In a version found on-line, the two parts have an additional title – *"The Tragedy"* and *"The Irony"*, which point up the message of the whole.

London is not a place usually associated with Hardy, who was born and spent much of his life in Dorset. However, he trained as an architect in London in his twenties and visited frequently. There is an account of the time he spent in London at www.the-tls.co.uk/articles/public/a-london-romance/. The evocation of London in this poem is at least as notable as that of the Wife – if not more so. This is a poem with a strong sense of *place*.

The poem has a variety of metric patterns, a mixture of three, four and two beat lines, but the pattern of each stanza is the same. Whilst the apparent irregularity gives it an uneasy feeling, as it does not settle into a regular beat, the overall regularity of the structure suggests a kind of inevitability.

I--The Tragedy

She sits in the tawny vapour
  That the City lanes have uprolled,
    Behind whose webby fold on fold
Like a waning taper
  The street-lamp glimmers cold.

The stanza heading prepares us for the emotional content of the verse, but the focus of this first stanza is very much on the Wife's surroundings – a foggy evening in London. This could also be seen as *pathetic fallacy* – the darkness and gloom mirroring the bad news that is about to be delivered. However, London was often smothered in fog at this time, from coal-fired homes and factories. The fog was a dirty yellow colour (*"tawny"*) as it contained particulates of soot, coal-dust and other pollutants. It was known as a *"pea-souper"* for its thickness and colour. The fog was so thick that it acted almost like a solid – a feature that other poets have exploited, as in TS Eliot's "<u>The Love-Song of J Alfred Prufrock</u>" (1920) which contains the lines:

The yellow fog that rubs its back upon the window-panes,
The yellow smoke that rubs its muzzle on the window-panes,
Licked its tongue into the corners of the evening,
Lingered upon the pools that stand in drains,
Let fall upon its back the soot that falls from chimneys,
Slipped by the terrace, made a sudden leap,
And seeing that it was a soft October night,
Curled once about the house, and fell asleep.

Fog like this persisted right through until the 1950s, when the first Clean Air Act was introduced, forbidding the burning of coal in homes.

The fog has rolled up from the City of London, probably up hill to the suburbs (the City is in the Thames river-valley, which would have added to the density of the fog). It is described as *"webby"* suggesting it is clinging and sticky like a spider's web. The streetlamps, which would have been gaslights, are seen as dimly as if they were candles. *"Cold"* adds to the dreariness of the evening, as the faint light brings no comfort.

A messenger's knock cracks smartly,
    Flashed news is in her hand
    Of meaning it dazes to understand
Though shaped so shortly:
    He--has fallen--in the far South Land . . .

The Wife receives a telegram – a short message sent, most probably by 1899 in London, electronically. The use of *"flashed"* harks back to an earlier time when messages were sent by means of Morse code and flashing lights – the pattern of "On" and "Off" spelling out letters. Telegrams were received by a Telegraph Office and delivered by hand. They came to be well-known as bearers of bad news, as their use suggested that the message was too urgent to be delivered by the normal postal system – which at this time, was significantly faster than modern day post. There is some irony in the contrast between the efficiency (*"cracks smartly"*) and speed (*"flashed"*), with which the message is delivered, emphasised by the *consonance*[21] (*"knock/cracks"*) and *assonance*[22] (*"cracks/flashed/hand"*), and the suggestion that it simply appears in her hand, (*"is in"*) without intermediary, and the Wife's dazed incomprehension of a message she would rather have not received at all, let alone with such haste. The abruptness of the message is conveyed in the *alliterated* and clipped "*shaped so shortly*", whilst the *hyphenation*, in contrast, draws out the final line, reproducing her puzzlement as she tries to grasp the meaning of the text – her husband has died in the Boer War in Africa.

II--The Irony

'Tis the morrow; the fog hangs thicker,
    The postman nears and goes:
        A letter is brought whose lines disclose
By the firelight flicker
        His hand, whom the worm now knows:

The irony of the title is created by the different speeds of communication between the telegram and the post. The next day she receives a letter through the post from her husband, written and sent while he was still alive, but overtaken by the telegram announcing his death. This time the news is delivered leisurely – the fog is thicker, slowing movement, the postman "*nears and goes*", almost unremarked, the rhythm suggesting a leisurely "to-ing and fro-ing". The letter is brought to her by someone else,

---

[21] Repeated or alliterated consonants
[22] Repeated or rhyming vowels

"The Darkling Thrush" – Thomas Hardy

Browning's *"first, fine, careless rapture"* from *"Home Thoughts, from Abroad"* is heard again here, but with a very different effect. The title alone suggests a more sombre note – the thrush is *"Darkling"* as it is singing as it grows dark, the dark being a metaphor for the end of the year, the end of the century (it was written in early 1900) and the end of the certainties of the Victorian era. *"Darkling"* also is a word much used by poets – most notably Keats (in another poem written to a bird – *"Ode to a Nightingale"* - in which he describes his mood as *"Darkling"*) and, closer to Hardy in time, Matthew Arnold. In his famous poem, *"On Dover Beach"* (publ. 1867), which is also in the anthology, Arnold writes:

*And we are here as on **a darkling plain***
Swept with confused alarms of struggle and flight
Where ignorant armies clash by night.

Arnold's answer to this bleak vision of mankind is to be *"true to one another"*.

An atheist from an early age, Hardy was nevertheless spiritual in his search for meaning in life, his desire to understand the forces working for good and evil among mankind, and his belief in the power of redemption through love and fellow feeling. *"The Darkling Thrush"* seems also to find Hardy at his lowest ebb, writing at the end of the 19th century, whilst the Boer War dragged on, and contemplating a doubtful future. Hardy had a deep, spiritual connection to the English landscape; in his novels, like *"Return of the Native"* or *"Tess"*, the Wessex countryside is as important as the characters. For Hardy to personify the landscape as a dead corpse is testimony to the depth of Hardy's despair.

The poem is in *common* metre with alternating *iambic tetrametre* and *iambic trimetre* lines, with the expected regular *ababcdcd* rhyme scheme. This may seem an odd choice for a poem which is non-narrative and lyrical. However, it is the contrast between the potentially jaunty rhythm and rhyme, and the darkness of the subject matter, as well as the manipulation of the *syntax* to emphasise particular words, and match the natural rhythm of speech to the regular metric line, that make the poem so effective.

I leant upon a coppice gate
    When Frost was spectre-grey,
And Winter's dregs made desolate
    The weakening eye of day.

The poet is out at twilight in winter and stops on his walk to rest, leaning on a gate which leads to a small wood (*"coppice"*). The first stanza depicts the frozen, empty landscape which is quickly imbued with a feeling of dread. The *"Frost"*, personified by the capitalisation to suggest its pervasive power, as is *"Winter"*, is like a ghost (*"spectre-grey"*); *"dregs"* means what is left over and has no goodness; the sun is pale and warmth less (*"weakening eye"*) and also *"desolate"*, like a blind sightless thing. Notice how the regular *iambic* rhythm is present, but made barely noticeable by the matching of the *iamb* to the words "made **de**solate" and the use of a *dactyl*[24] on "**wea**kening **eye**", which match speech rhythms.

The tangled bine-stems scored the sky
    Like strings of broken lyres,
And all mankind that haunted nigh
    Had sought their household fires.

---

[24] A metric foot which has a **TUM** - ti-ti (heavy light light) beat

Not only is this landscape cheerless, but the imagery in the next four lines suggests that the world itself is "out of tune". *"tangled bine stems"* are the curling tendrils of a plant – possibly *woodbine* or honeysuckle, a climbing plant which entangles itself in low bushes and trees – which can be seen against the leafless branches. The lyre is a stringed instrument from classical Greece (from which the word *"lyric"* comes) which lifts this very English scene into the realm of the time less and universal. The word *"scored"*, here meaning to make deep cuts, another bleak image, may also be a punning reference to music. This universality is reinforced by the use of *"mankind"*, rather than *"men"*. The use of *"haunted"* rather than *"lived"* again suggests that, as Hamlet says, *"the time is out of joint"*, at odds with itself.

The land's sharp features seemed to be
    The Century's corpse outleant,
His crypt the cloudy canopy,
    The wind his death-lament.
The ancient pulse of germ and birth
    Was shrunken hard and dry,
And every spirit upon earth
    Seemed fervourless as I.

The imagery of death and decay continues, transforming the English landscape into the stuff of nightmares. He sees the land before him as the embodiment of the 19th century, which has just "died". *"Outleant"* appears to be a *neologism*[25] by Hardy, presumably meaning "lent out", as if the dying century has inhabited the landscape and died there, its *"features"* thin and wasted to show the *"sharp"* bones beneath. The tomb of the Century is the leaden grey, cloud-covered sky and the shrieking of the winter wind the wailing of mourners. The *alliterated* *"crypt/cloudy/canopy"* suggests the hard edges of a stone tomb.

---

[25] A newly made or *"coined"* word

The life-force of the land - *"germ"* means "seed" – is shrivelled up. Mankind wanders this barren landscape as a homeless spirit, aimless and energy-less – as Hardy does. Overall, it is vision of decay and hopelessness, with him at the epicentre.

At once a voice arose among
  The bleak twigs overhead
In a full-hearted evensong
  Of joy illimited;
An aged thrush, frail, gaunt, and small,
  In blast-beruffled plume,
Had chosen thus to fling his soul
  Upon the growing gloom.

Suddenly, the silence is broken by a *"voice"*. Whose is not yet known, as if Hardy is searching for the source in the *"bleak twigs overhead"*. The "l" sound in *"bleak"* is the first in a series of alliterated "*l*" sounds that continue throughout the stanza. The transformation that this *"voice"* brings, however, is immediately apparent – it is *"full-hearted"*, in contrast to the lifeless corpses wandering around, and it sings an *"evensong"*, here meaning a "song sung in the evening", but also the religious service held daily in church, suggestive of people coming together. The trilling sound of *"illimited"*, another word coined by Hardy, suggests the bird's song and the alliterated *"l"* continues over the next five lines: *"illimited/frail/small/blast/beruffled/plume/fling /soul/ gloom"* in an outpouring of song. This is a similar use of alliterated "*l*" as Charlotte Bronte's evocation of the caged canary in *"The house was still..."*. The thrush is *"aged"* – like the century has aged - until it seems to be barely hanging on to life; it is being battered by the wind. There is a poignant contrast between the force of the wind in the *plosive*[26] *"blast"* and the softness and

---

[26] Sounds made by the letter *"b"*, *"p"*, *"t"* etc.

fragility of *"beruffled plume"*. None of this, however, can stop him singing his heart out.

> *So little cause for carolings*
> > *Of such ecstatic sound*
> *Was written on terrestrial things*
> > *Afar or nigh around,*
> *That I could think there trembled through*
> > *His happy good-night air*
> *Some blessed Hope, whereof he knew*
> > *And I was unaware.*

Hardy reflects on why this bird should choose to sing (*"carolings"* again suggests harmony between people, as they come together to sing) with such joyous abandon, in a landscape which gives no encouragement to it. The song *"trembles"*, a reference to the trilling sound, but also to the contrast between the inhospitality of the bird's surroundings and the fragility of his singing, as if the *"darkling"* forces might prevail. There is also something very simple, innocent and child-like about the phrase *"happy good-night air"* as well as another typical Hardy punning association – between *"good-night"* as in "farewell" and *"good night"* as in pleasant. The only conclusion Hardy can come to is that the bird knows a reason for being joyous in the face of all this despair – a Hope for the future – which is hidden from Hardy.

Whether this poem ends on a note of optimism or pessimism is moot. Is the thrush a *"wise thrush"*, as in Browning's poem, knowing better than us, being in tune with the world and his place in it, and hence, full of *"rapture"*? Or is he merely a bird that knows nothing of the troubles that beset mankind and is merely a *"waking dream"* as Keats wonders about his *Nightingale*? Does Hardy go away from the scene uplifted by the thrush's song – or does he remain ignorant of the reason for it? There may be a clue in the use of *"communion"* and *"carolling"* in the evocation of communal singing – perhaps Matthew Arnold's answer, *"be true to one another"*, has resonance for Hardy as well.

Printed in Great Britain
by Amazon